Also by Julia Child

Mastering the Art of French Cooking, Volume I
(with Simone Beck and Louisette Bertholle)

The French Chef Cookbook

Mastering the Art of French Cooking, Volume II
(with Simone Beck)

From Julia Child's Kitchen

The Way to Cook

Cooking with Master Chefs

In Julia's Kitchen with Master Chefs

Julia's Casual Dinners

Julia's Casual Dinners

by Julia Child

In collaboration with E. S. Yntema

Photographs by James Scherer

Alfred A. Knopf   New York   1999

This Is a Borzoi Book
Published by Alfred A. Knopf, Inc.

The recipes in this book were originally published in the
books *Julia Child & Company* and *Julia Child & More
Company,* which were published by Alfred A. Knopf,
Inc., in 1978 and 1979 respectively. *Julia Child & Company* copyright © 1978 and *Julia Child & More Company* copyright © 1979 by Julia Child. These two books
were also released in a single edition as *Julia Child's
Menu Cookbook,* published in 1991 by Wings Books,
distributed by Outlet Book Company, Inc., a Random
House Company, by arrangement with Alfred A.
Knopf, Inc.

"UFOs in Wine" appeared in somewhat shorter form in
McCall's.

Library of Congress Cataloging-in-Publication Data
Child, Julia.
   Julia's casual dinners / by Julia Child, in collaboration
with E. S. Yntema ; photographs by James Scherer. —
1st ed.
     p.   cm.
   Includes index.
   ISBN 0-375-40337-X
   1. Cookery.   2. Menus.   I. Yntema, E. S.   II. Title.
TX715.C545624   1999
642'.4—dc21   98-38188
                                                    CIP

Manufactured in the United States of America
First Edition

Contents

Acknowledgments

This is a book of menus drawn from our television series *Julia Child & Company* and its sequel, *Julia Child & More Company*. The recipes for the complete series appeared in two separate books, were then all collected into one big book, and are now split into four convenient smaller books, of which this is the third volume.

The series was produced for public television at WGBH TV in Boston with Russell Morash as producer/director in association with Ruth Lockwood. The food designer and recipe developer was Rosemary Manell, who worked closely with our photographer, James Scherer. Marian Morash, chef for the popular *This Old House,* was also executive chef for us. I count us fortunate indeed to have had E. S. Yntema as a writer. Peggy Yntema's wit and spirit always make for good reading.

It takes a peck of people to put on shows such as these, and other members of our team at one time or another included Gladys Christopherson, Bess Coughlin, Wendy Davidson, Bonnie Eleph, Jo Ford, Temi Hyde, Sara Moulton, Pat Pratt, John Reardon, Bev Seamons, and, of course, our able makeup artist, Louise Miller. I have not mentioned the technicians, camera crew, and lighting engineers, or our book designer, Chris Pullman, or our favorite editor at Knopf, Judith Jones.

Introduction

Menu books are useful to have on hand since you can use them for complete dinners — literally from soup to nuts — where you are escorted step by step, or you can pluck out single dishes. This third book in our series gives you everything from a pep talk at the beginning of the menu to the shopping list, the order of battle, complete recipes for each dish plus variations and alternates, and suggestions on which wines go with what foods. Follow faithfully and you don't even have to think. Or you may want to substitute your own famous spinach recipe for the green beans suggested, or your special and sumptuous *Riz á L'Impératrice* for the Floating Island in the menu.

That Floating Island, however, is a very special dessert and one that's useful to have in your repertoire since you can ready the parts a day or two in advance, and it is the kind of finale that will go with almost any meal. This particular meal, Informal Dinner, includes a beautiful roast of veal that is slowly braised in a covered casserole with aromatic vegetables, producing its own fragrant sauce as all the elements slowly release and mingle their particular flavors. A sauté of grated zucchini and spinach completes the course. The dinner begins with a modest serving of crisp puff pastry rectangles filled with fresh asparagus tips and a dollop of lemon butter sauce. The Floating Island makes an attractive light finish, and is always a conversation piece. But you might prefer a fruit dessert, such as the orange and blueberry bowl in the UFOs in Wine dinner. The UFOs, by the way, are Rock Cornish game hens, broil-roasted with wine and cheese and served on a giant cake of sautéed shredded potatoes.

The Buffet for 19 offers some easily expandable dishes, from its turkey Orloff casserole with cheese, mushrooms, onions, and rice to its Jamaican ice cream goblet, where rum and coffee sprinkles cleverly garnish store-bought ice cream. When you want A Fast Fish Dinner we suggest you begin with a chilled beet and cucumber soup, which your food processor will make for you literally in a flash, puréeing cooked or canned beets and raw cucumbers. When you top each bowl with a splash of sour cream and some fresh dill you have made yourself an instant borscht. Monkfish tails are sautéed quickly, then briefly simmered in a julienne of colorful peppers and onions. The dessert is my favorite lemon flan.

A host of fine dishes awaits you here, from the very simple sauté of cherry tomatoes to the elaborately decorated crust for the *pâté en croûte,* and from basic mashed potatoes to that glorious chocolate creation, the *Gâteau Victoire.* May you enjoy these menus!

Bon Appétit!

Julia Child

1998

🕐 *indicates stop here*
▼ *indicates further discussion under Remarks*

Julia's Casual Dinners

Beautiful ingredients prepared with loving care but little effort: this simple menu is an example of the wisdom and sane good taste of civilized cookery.

Informal Dinner

Menu

Asparagus Tips in Puff Pastry, Lemon Butter Sauce

ॐ

Casserole Roast of Veal with Carrots and Celery Hearts
Wok Sauté of Grated Zucchini and Fresh Spinach

ॐ

Floating Island

ॐ

Suggested wines:
A light white wine with the first course, like a Chablis, Chardonnay, or dry Riesling; a red Bordeaux or Cabernet Sauvignon with the veal; a Champagne or sparkling white wine with the dessert

"Love and work," said Sigmund Freud when somebody asked him what he thought were the most important things in life. Not much work goes into cooking the ingredients for this simple, beautiful dinner. But in choosing them you acknowledge your guests' love of perfection and exercise your own.

You could spend half the money this menu demands and create a meal twice as impressive. There are several such menus in this book, and very good they are, too. But if your trusted butcher lets you know that he has been able to procure a veal roast of impeccable quality, wouldn't you plan to share it with friends who will appreciate its rarity? Wouldn't you go to market that morning for the freshest vegetables, imagining which ones would contribute to the flavor of the meat?

This serene, unpretentious perfection in dining is, indeed, the reward of love, expressed by care and respect for your guests and for the food you offer them. And if veal really is too expensive for you—or impossible to come by— try one of the less luxurious meats suggested in Menu Variations; the substitutes are perfectly suited to this kind of cooking method and will have a fine harmony of flavors.

A casserole is a very comfortable kind of informal cooking. You simply brown the meat, briefly blanch the vegetables, and put them all together with butter and seasonings. Then, when you're ready to roast, you stick the casserole in the oven and let it cook quietly by itself, once in a while basting the meat and vegetables with their communal juices while you go about other things. The fresh, slightly crunchy spinach and zucchini, only lightly cooked at the last minute, will complete a pretty plateful and make a salad unnecessary.

What's a Chinese wok doing at this very traditional meal? Improving it, that's what, and reminding us not to be pedantic...but you could use a frying pan.

The main course doesn't include rice or potatoes, but it doesn't need to if you serve a loaf of French bread. And you may not even need that because of the appetizer. These crinkly little puff pastry "rafts" are all the rage these days in France; but puff pastry was never an everyday item there, any more than here, until recently. With a new fast method (see Appendix, page 111), puff pastry dishes are almost effortless, once you get the habit of making a batch of dough at intervals and cutting some of it into handy little rectangles to await your convenience in the freezer. Asparagus, formerly such a luxury, is available here from February through June at gradually decreasing prices. You need only three or four spears per person. Peel them, of course, or the dish is hardly

worth presenting. And, to round out the delicate contrast of texture and flavor, whisk up a last-minute little sauce.

Be careful the butter doesn't overheat; be careful the asparagus doesn't overcook; be careful your oven thermostat is accurate. Cooking, I do strongly feel, expresses love more by fastidious everyday care than by festival bursts of effort. The effort, when you come to the dessert, can be left to your heavy-duty mixer. If you had to do this by hand, it would indeed be heavy duty.

Floating island, as the French do it, is a meringue soufflé about the size of Australia, floating on a sea of pale-gold custard sauce. I like to serve it in archipelago form, cut into Greenland-size chunks. Don't be daunted at this point by the word "soufflé," in case you aren't yet confident with them: this meringue is so foolproof you can unmold it any time, or even put it in the freezer. The custard sauce, too, can be made well in advance, and it is very easy, provided you give it the few minutes' close attention (to prevent its curdling) that this lovely satiny confection deserves.

"Make every meal an occasion" sounds to me like "Live each day as though it were your last"—just plain overwrought. People do preach it, but does anyone practice? Not me! But to love your art as well as your audience does seem to make for pretty good living, day by pleasant day.

Preparations

Recommended Equipment:
A wok is not essential for the zucchini and spinach dish, just an attractive option. But I would not tackle 12 egg whites without a big electric mixer and an appropriate bowl (see recipe).

Marketing and Storage:
Staples to have on hand

Salt
Black and white peppercorns
Cream of tartar
Pure vanilla extract
Fragrant dried tarragon
Light olive oil or fresh peanut oil ▼
Granulated sugar
Optional but recommended: superfine
   granulated sugar

Butter (¾ pound or 350 g)
Milk (1 pint or 2 cups or ½ L)
Eggs (13 or more, depending on size)
Onions (2)
Lemons (1)
Puff pastry (from the freezer)
Shallots or scallions
Dry white French vermouth
Optional: dark Jamaica rum or
   bourbon whiskey

Specific ingredients for this menu

Boneless roast of veal (3 pounds or 1¼ to
   1½ kg); please read the recipe
   before marketing
Fresh pork fat (or beef fat) ▼
Fresh asparagus (18 to 24 spears)
Fresh celery hearts (3 to 6 whole)
Fresh carrots (6 to 8 or more)
Zucchini (6 medium-size)
Fresh spinach (1½ to 2 pounds or ¾ to 1 kg)
Optional: heavy cream (2 to 4 Tb)
Optional: sprinkles for meringue (see recipe)

▶ *Remarks:*

Staples

Fresh peanut oil: Peanut oil can get rancid, so sniff yours before using.

Ingredients for this menu

Fresh pork fat: "Barding" fat, to cover a lean roast, is not always sold; so whenever I see some I buy it and freeze it. And I trim scraps of extra fat off pork roasts before cooking, and save them. If the strips you buy are too thick, place between sheets of wax paper and pound with a rubber hammer, rolling pin, or bottle to flatten them out. You can substitute fat trimmed from a beef loin or rib roast; it does the work, although not as neatly since it shrinks and tends to break as it cooks.

Asparagus Tips in Puff Pastry, Lemon Butter Sauce

Petites Feuilletées aux Asperges, Sauce Beurre au Citron

For 6 people as a first course

18 to 24 fresh asparagus spears (depending on size)

2 to 3 Tb butter and 1 Tb minced shallots or scallions

Salt and pepper

6 puff pastry rectangles about 2½ by 5 by ¼ inches or 6½ by 13 by ¾ cm (the recipe for French puff pastry is on page 111)

Egg glaze (1 egg beaten with 1 tsp water)

Lemon butter sauce

2 Tb fresh lemon juice

3 Tb dry white French vermouth

Salt and white pepper

1 stick (115 g) chilled butter cut into 12 fingertip-size pieces

The asparagus

Trim ends off asparagus spears and peel from butt to near tip to remove tough outer skin. Choose a deep skillet or oval flameproof casserole large enough to hold asparagus flat; fill with water and bring to the rolling boil, adding 1½ teaspoons salt per quart or liter of water. Lay in the asparagus, cover until boil is reached, then uncover and boil slowly just until asparagus is cooked through—5 to 8 minutes or so, depending on quality (eat a piece off the butt end of one to make sure). Immediately remove the asparagus and arrange in one layer on a clean towel to cool. Cut the tip ends of the spears into 5-inch (13-cm) lengths; save the butt ends for a salad.

🕐   May be cooked in advance. When cold, wrap and refrigerate.

Just before serving (and when the following pastry is baked and ready), melt 2 to 3 tablespoons butter in a frying pan large enough to hold the tips in one layer, add the shallots or scallions and cook for a moment, then add the asparagus tips, shaking pan by handle to roll them over and over to coat with butter; season lightly with salt and pepper and roll again.

The puff pastry rectangles

Preheat oven to 450°F/230°C. About 15 minutes before serving, arrange the pastries (still frozen, if you wish) on a baking sheet and paint the tops (not the sides) with egg glaze; in a moment, paint with a second coat, then make decorative knife cuts and crosshatchings in the surface. Immediately bake in middle level of oven for 12 to 15 minutes, until pastries have puffed up and browned and the sides have crisped.

🕐   May be baked somewhat ahead and left in turned-off oven, door ajar—but the sooner you serve them the more tenderly flakily buttery they will be.

To serve

While they are still hot, split the pastries in half horizontally, arrange 3 or 4 hot and buttery asparagus spears on the bottom half, their tips peeking out one of the ends, spoon a bit of the following sauce over the asparagus, cover loosely with the top, and serve at once.

Lemon butter sauce: an informal *beurre blanc* (which takes only 3 to 4 minutes to make; if you are not familiar with it, I suggest you do so just before serving since it is tricky to keep). Boil the lemon juice, vermouth, and ¼ teaspoon salt slowly in a small saucepan until liquid has reduced to about 1 tablespoon. Then, a piece or two at a time, start beating in the chilled pieces of butter, adding another piece or two just as the previous pieces have almost melted—the object here is to force its milk solids to hold in creamy suspension as the butter warms and softens, so that the sauce remains ivory colored rather than looking like melted butter. Season to taste with salt and pepper.

🕐   Sauce can be held over the faint heat of a pilot light or anywhere it is warm enough to keep the butter from congealing, but not so warm as to turn the sauce into melted butter. However, if this happens you can often bring it back by beating over cold water until it begins to congeal and cream again.

Remarks:

Jacques Pépin, the able French chef and teacher based in Connecticut, has another version of the sauce where you bring 2 tablespoons each of lemon juice and water to the rolling boil and rapidly beat in 1 stick (115 g) of soft butter in pieces; bring the sauce to the rolling boil again for a few seconds, turn into a sauce boat, and serve at once. It produces the same effect of a warm creamy liaison of butter, rather than melted butter.

Puff pastry rectangle before and after baking

Casserole Roast of Veal with Carrots and Celery Hearts

Rôti de Veau Poêlé à la Nivernaise

A fine roast of veal of top quality has no pronounced flavor of its own and no natural fat to keep it moist while it is cooking. I therefore like to tie my veal roast with strips of fat and to roast it slowly in a covered casserole with herbs and aromatic vegetables. As it cooks, the aroma of its savory companions seeps into the meat and the meat itself flavors the vegetables, both exuding a modicum of fragrant juices which combine to make a spontaneous sauce.

For 6 to 8 people

A 3-pound (1¼–1½ kg) boneless roast of veal, of the finest quality and palest pink (see notes on veal at end of recipe)

Strips of fresh pork fat (or beef fat) to tie around roast (about ⅛ inch or ½ cm thick and enough to cover half of the roast)

Light olive oil or fresh peanut oil, for browning meat

3 to 6 celery hearts

6 to 8 or more carrots

1 medium-size onion, sliced

Salt and pepper

1 tsp fragrant dried tarragon

2 Tb melted butter

Equipment

White butcher's string; a heavy covered casserole or roaster just large enough to hold meat and vegetables comfortably; a bulb baster; a meat thermometer

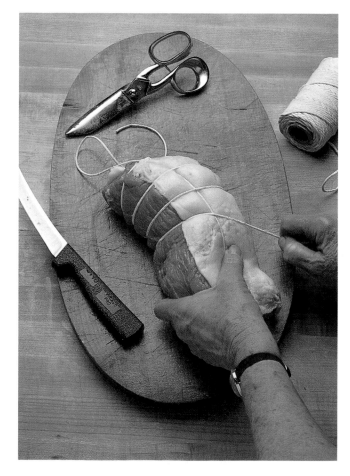

Preliminaries to roasting

Dry the veal in paper towels and tie the fat in place over it so you have strips on both top and bottom of veal. Film a frying pan or bottom of casserole with oil and brown the meat slowly over moderately high heat. Meanwhile cut the celery hearts into 5-inch (13-cm) lengths and reserve tops for another recipe. Trim celery roots, being careful not to detach ribs from them, and trim any bruised spots off ribs. Cut into halves or thirds lengthwise and wash under cold water, spreading ribs carefully apart to force sand and dirt out from around root end. Set aside. Peel the carrots and cut into thickish bias slices about 2½ inches (6½ cm) long. Drop both celery and carrots into a large pan of boiling salted water and blanch (boil) for 1 minute; drain.

Arranging the casserole

If you have browned the meat in the casserole, remove it and discard browning fat. Strew the onion slices in the bottom of the casserole, season the veal with a good sprinkling of salt and pepper, and place in casserole, a fat-stripped side up. Sprinkle on half the tarragon, and arrange the celery hearts on either side of roast. Sprinkle hearts with salt and a pinch of tarragon, then strew the carrots on top, seasoning them also. Baste with the melted butter.

🕐   Casserole may be arranged several hours before roasting.

Roasting the meat

Roasting time: 1¼ to 1½ hours
Preheat oven to 350°F/180°C. About 2 hours before you wish to serve (reheat casserole on top of the stove if you have arranged it ahead), set casserole in lower middle level of preheated oven. Roast for 20 minutes, then rapidly baste meat and vegetables with accumulated juices (a bulb baster is best for this) and turn thermostat down to 325°F/170°C. Baste every 20 minutes, and when an hour is up begin checking meat temperature. Meat is done at 165–170°F/75–77°C.

🕐   May be roasted somewhat ahead but should be kept warm; set cover slightly askew and keep in turned-off oven with door ajar, or over almost simmering water, or at a temperature of 120°F/50°C.

Serving

Slice the veal into thin, even pieces and arrange down the center of a hot platter, with the carrots bordering the meat and the celery hearts ringing them. Baste meat and vegetables with a little of the casserole juices. Spoon accumulated fat off remaining juices, correct seasoning, and strain into a hot sauce bowl.

Notes on Veal:

Veal is the meat of a young calf, and the best or Prime quality comes from an animal 10 to 12 weeks old that has been fed on milk or milk by-products. It is of the palest pink in color and has both texture and flavor—although the flavor of veal is never robust, like that of lamb or beef. Such veal is very expensive indeed but produces beautiful boneless cuts of solid meat from the leg (such as the top round) and from the loin and rib. Younger and less expensive veal, which should also be of the palest pink in color, is usually too small to furnish top or bottom round cuts, so one should take the whole leg and either roast it as is or have it boned and tied.

Wok Sauté of Grated Zucchini and Fresh Spinach

Sauté de Courgettes, Viroflay

In this attractive combination, the fresh spinach gives character to the zucchini, and the zucchini tenderizes the bite of the spinach, while a little onion lends its subtle depth. Although you can cook it all in a frying pan, the wok is especially successful here.

For 6 people

| 6 medium-size zucchini |
| Salt |
| 1½ to 2 pounds (¾–1 kg) fresh spinach |

2 to 3 Tb light olive oil or fresh peanut oil

3 to 4 Tb butter

1 medium-size onion, sliced

Pepper

Equipment

A food processor (optional) for grating the zucchini—or the coarse side of a hand grater; a wok (also optional), preferably with stainless-steel or nonstick interior so that spinach will not pick up a metallic taste

Trim off the ends and scrub the zucchini under cold water, but do not peel them. Grate either in a processor or through a hand grater and place in a sieve set over a bowl; toss with a teaspoon of salt and let drain while you trim the spinach.

Pull the stems off the spinach and pump leaves up and down in a basin of cold water, draining and repeating process if necessary to be sure spinach contains no sand or dirt. Drain in a colander.

🕐 May be prepared several hours in advance; refrigerate if you are not proceeding with recipe.

When you are ready to sauté, heat 1 tablespoon of oil and 1½ tablespoons butter in the wok (or frying pan). When butter has melted, add the spinach (if spinach is dry, add also 2 to 3 tablespoons water). Toss and turn for 5 minutes or so, until spinach is wilted and just cooked through, then remove it to a side dish. While spinach is cooking, by handfuls squeeze the juices out of the zucchini and set on a plate. When spinach is done and out of the wok, add more oil and butter and the sliced onion. Toss and cook for a minute or two, then add the zucchini, tossing and turning it for several minutes, until just tender. Press any accumulated liquid out of spinach, and toss spinach with

zucchini, tossing and turning for a minute or two to blend and heat the two vegetables together. Taste carefully for seasoning, adding salt and pepper as needed, and you are ready to serve.

🕐 Most of the cooking may be done in advance, but in this case cook the spinach and set aside, then cook the zucchini until almost tender; finish the cooking just before serving, then add the spinach, tossing and turning for a moment or two.

Remarks:

You could add several tablespoons of heavy cream near the end of the cooking, or enrich the vegetables with more butter at the end of the cooking. Alternatively, you can cook with oil only, or use less of the amounts of both butter and oil specified in the recipe—that is the versatility of cooking in a well-designed wok.

Pulling the stems off spinach leaves

Squeezing the juices out of grated raw zucchini

Floating Island

Ile Flottante—A giant meringue soufflé floating on a custard sea

Here is a dramatic yet light and lovely cold dessert that is simplicity itself to make when you have a well-designed electric mixer that will keep the whole mass of your egg whites in motion at once, so that you get the lightness and volume egg whites should produce.

For 6 to 8 people

1⅔ cups (3¾ dL) egg whites (about 12)

½ tsp cream of tartar and 1/16 tsp salt

1½ cups (3½ dL) sugar (preferably the very finely granulated or instant kind)

2 tsp pure vanilla extract

3 cups (¾ L) Custard Sauce (see notes at end of recipe)

4 to 5 Tb decorative sprinkles for top of meringue, as suggested in Serving paragraph below (optional)

Equipment

(Besides the mixer): a 4- to 5-quart (4- to 4¾-L) straight-sided baking dish or casserole, interior heavily buttered and dusted with sugar; a round flat platter for unmolding

Cautionary remarks

Be sure that your egg-beating bowl and beater blades are absolutely clean and dry, since any oil or grease on them will prevent the egg whites from mounting. Also, because you are separating so many eggs, it is a good idea to break the whites, one at a time, into a small clean bowl and add each as you do it to the beating bowl; then, if you break a yolk, it will ruin only one egg white, not the whole batch (since specks of egg yolk can prevent the whites from rising). Finally, chilled egg whites will not mount properly; stir them in the mixing bowl over hot water until the chill is off and they are about the temperature of your finger.

The meringue mixture

Preheat oven to 250°F/130°C. Start beating the egg whites at moderately slow speed until they are foamy. Beat in the cream of tartar and salt and gradually increase speed to fast. When the egg whites form soft peaks, sprinkle in the sugar (decreasing speed if necessary) by 4-spoonful dollops until all is added, then beat at high speed for several minutes until egg whites form stiff shining peaks. Beat in the vanilla. Scoop the meringue into the prepared baking dish, which should be almost filled (but do not worry if dish is only three-quarters full—it makes no difference).

Baking the meringue

Immediately set the dish in the lower middle level of your preheated oven and bake 35 to 40 minutes, or until the meringue has souffléed (or risen) 2 to 3 inches (5 to 8 cm) and a skewer plunged through the side of the puff down to the bottom of the dish comes out clean. If necessary, bake 4 to 5 minutes or so more—a very little too much is better than too little. Remove from oven and set at room temperature for 30 minutes or until cool; it will sink down to somewhat less than its original volume, and will eventually shrink from sides of dish. When cool, cover and refrigerate.

🕐 May be baked several hours or even a day or two in advance; may even be frozen.

Serving

(You may unmold it onto a round platter, pour your custard sauce around, and serve as is, or use the following system.) Run a thin knife around edge of dish to detach meringue, then push the whole meringue gently with a rubber spatula all around to make sure bottom is not sticking. Turn a flat round dish, like a pizza pan, upside down over baking dish and reverse the two, giving a slap and a downward jerk to dislodge meringue onto round dish. Pour a good layer of custard sauce into a round platter, cut large wedges out of the meringue with a pie server, and arrange in the custard. Just before serving, sprinkle the meringue wedges, if you wish, with pulverized nut brittle, crumbled macaroons, or toasted ground nuts.

Custard Sauce:

You will need about 3 cups (¾ L), with 6 egg yolks, ⅔ cup (1½ dL) sugar, 1½ cups (3½ dL) milk, 1½ tablespoons pure vanilla extract, plus an addition I like with this dessert—3 to 4 tablespoons dark Jamaica rum or bourbon whiskey—and 3 to 4 tablespoons unsalted butter beaten in at the end.

⏱ *Timing*

When we're "just family," or have invited guests to dine informally, we often eat in the kitchen so that last-minute jobs don't interrupt the conversation. With this menu, which does involve some final touches, we'd surely eat there. Before sitting down, one must turn the asparagus in butter; and, since the little sauce is tricky to keep warm, it's a good idea to make it at the last minute. And the spinach and zucchini dish is at its best if you finish its cooking, a matter of moments, just before eating it. The veal and vegetable platter takes only a minute to arrange, so do it on the spot.

The puff pastry is best when just baked, which takes no more than 15 minutes. I'd remove mine from the freezer and slip it into the preheated oven just about halfway through our apéritifs or cocktails.

Otherwise, this meal puts only slight demands on your time. Two hours before dinner, start cooking your casserole. You can arrange it in the morning; and that's when, ideally, you'd shop for the freshest asparagus, spinach, and zucchini. You can boil the asparagus then and precook the wok vegetables.

Both the custard sauce and the meringue, though the latter looks so ethereal, can be made and refrigerated a day or so ahead, and the puff pastry dough, any time at all.

Menu Variations

The appetizer: Inside a hot split piece of puff pastry, you can place a creamed shellfish mixture, sauced wild mushrooms or chicken livers, or—using the butter sauce—substitute peeled broccoli flowerettes for the asparagus, or spears of peeled and seeded cucumber cooked in butter with chopped shallots and herbs. Instead of pastry, you can use hard-toasted bread (*croûtes*), and a nice way to make them crisp and rich is to butter sliced crustless bread on both sides and bake till golden in a moderate oven. Or hollow out two-finger-thick rectangles of unsliced white bread, butter tops, sides, and insides, and brown in the oven for *croustades.*

The casserole roast: A boned loin of pork roast works beautifully in this recipe, as does a boneless half turkey breast. Though the slices will be inelegant, you can keep that lovely veal flavor by using a cheaper cut, boned and rolled. Or substitute a boneless cut of beef; but use only meat of roasting quality, like *filet*, sirloin strip, or extra-fine rump.

For aromatic vegetables which will hold their shape and color, think of such roots as onions, turnips, rutabaga, celery root, or oyster plant to combine with the likes of fennel, leeks, or endive. These flavors are strong, so adjust your herbs accordingly.

The wok sauté: For something leafy and green combined with something soft and succulent, one could substitute very young beet or turnip greens, young dandelion leaves, kale, or stemmed chard for the spinach; and for the zucchini, summer or pattypan squash, pumpkin, cucumber, or slivers of white turnip, which are remarkably good with spinach.

The dessert: The American form of floating island has little islets of meringue poached in milk afloat on a custard sauce flavored with vanilla only. I wouldn't use any custard-and-meringue variant involving cake or pastry, since it would be a little heavy, considering the pastry appetizer; but that still leaves a vast range, from the elegant sabayons (of which Zabaione Batardo Veneziano on page 53 is a cousin on the Bavarian cream side). There are mousses and flans and unmolded custards, simple cup custards baked or boiled; and you could even bake a meringue case with a custard filling and decorate it with fruit. You can make a charming fruit soufflé by adding a thick purée of fruit like prunes or apricots to the meringue mixture, in the proportion of 1 cup (¼ L) purée to 5 egg whites; this, of course, you serve hot. And there are many delicious cold "soufflés."

Leftovers

The casserole: The leftover vegetables, and all the juice, will be good additions to a soup. Cold sliced veal is excellent with a piquant sauce; add any scraps to a creamed dish.

The wok sauté: One delicious by-product is the bright-green juice extracted from the zucchini by the grater. If you add it to a soup, be careful with salt, as it contains a lot. Any leftover cooked zucchini and spinach would also be good in a soup; or use it as filling for omelets or quiche.

The dessert: You can refrigerate any leftovers and serve again the next day. Extra custard sauce can be frozen and is wonderful on all kinds of puddings, particularly Indian. Or you can stir in any leftover sprinklings, add chopped nuts and chopped candied fruit, and freeze, for a sort of biscuit tortoni. Extra baked meringue is pleasant with a fruit sauce—raspberry, for instance.

Wok sauté of spinach with turnips

Postscript

The French are given to classifying everything, usually on a scale of grandeur. In ascending degrees, cooking is divided into *la cuisine bonne femme* (goodwife), sometimes also termed *paysanne* or peasant; next step up, plain family cooking, or *la cuisine de famille;* then *la cuisine bourgeoise,* or fancy family cooking; and, finally, great, or high-class, cooking, *la grande* or *la haute cuisine.* The differences are not easy to define.

Perhaps some examples will help. If you have had dinner at midday and now make your supper on a hearty potato and leek soup taken with chunks of bread and a local wine and followed by a bowl of cherries, you are eating goodwife or peasant style—which I love to do. If your idea of a Sunday lunch is a starter of sliced tomatoes *vinaigrette,* then roast garlicky leg of lamb with green beans cooked in lard, then cheese, then perhaps an apple tart from the baker's, that's family cooking. Bourgeois cooking—a bit more sophisticated and expensive, but not showy and never eccentric—is exemplified by the menu in this chapter. Grand, or classy, cuisine really means the cooking of great chefs and grand restaurants: with its hierarchy of foundation stocks and sauces and flavored butters, its complexity, and, occasionally, its emphasis on display or on rare ingredients.

In her scholarly *Great Cooks and Their Recipes: From Taillevent to Escoffier* (New York: McGraw-Hill Book Company, 1977), Anne Willan cites Escoffier's turn-of-the-century recipe for Tournedos Chasseur as "a good example of the step-by-step preparation of *haute cuisine,* resulting here in a deceptively simple steak with wine sauce. The recipe requires four basic preparations—stock, demi-glace sauce, meat glaze…and tomato sauce—for the final sauce." *Demi-glace* and meat glaze, as she reminds us, are themselves cooked for hours and are composed of other, still more basic preparations. Nonetheless, the dish is "one of Escoffier's easier recipes for tournedos, with no elaborate garnish."

Cooking of such complexity will rarely be practical at home, though none of the four basic preparations is technically difficult; but other formerly *haute, grande,* and indeed formidable dishes are now perfectly manageable, thanks to the processor, the freezer, etc.

"In reality," wrote Escoffier, "practice dictates fixed and regular quantities, and from these one cannot diverge." He was writing about sauces, of which, in his *Guide Culinaire,* he described 136, not counting dessert sauces. The great codifier put enormous emphasis on correctness, hence predictability. In Escoffier's case, as in politics, his creativity and revolutionary work were succeeded by a long period of gradual rigidification; thirty years after his death in 1935, great chefs were following his dictates everywhere. If you ordered a dish in any great restaurant, you knew by its name precisely what you were getting. If, for instance, your *coulibiac* failed to contain *vesiga,* or a sturgeon's spinal marrow (a minor and almost unobtainable ingredient), then it wasn't *coulibiac* at all, and the chef had scandalously flouted the proprieties.

In the seventies, cooking was released from this straitjacket by the joyously anarchic *nouvelle cuisine,* whose most familiar exponent—to Americans—is Michel Guérard. Best known here for the ingenious diet recipes of *la cuisine minceur*—which is only one aspect of his work—Guérard is a classically trained chef of great sensitivity. His unprecedented combinations and piquant menus have inspired some bizarre travesties; but cooking has been liberated by his daring and original genius.

A natural rightness rather than a pedantic correctness is my goal in cooking. And in composing a menu—or a dish—nobody's codes or classifications have any bearing whatever, so far as I'm concerned. One turns with relief from words to realities.

Advance preparation, easy service, and a charming main dish adapted from a classic of the haute cuisine; *special treats for a big crowd.*

Buffet for 19

Menu

Oysters on the Half Shell

❦

Turkey Orloff—turkey breast scallopini gratinéed with mushrooms, onions, rice, and cheese
Fresh Green Beans with Watercress and Tomatoes, Oil and Lemon Dressing
French Bread

❦

Jamaican Ice Cream Goblet

❦

Suggested wines:
Chablis, Muscadet, or Riesling with the oysters; red Bordeaux or Cabernet Sauvignon with the turkey

Supper for a crowd nowadays means buffet service. I ask of a good buffet main dish that it be easy to serve, hold heat well, be reasonably compact to save oven and table space, that it be neither expensive nor pretentious, and that it may be prepared largely in advance. At once I add: the dish must be delicious, handsome, and a little unusual. Just because the guests have been invited en masse, they mustn't be let think that their dinner has been indifferently chosen or perfunctorily prepared.

None of the menus in this book requires a special setting or unusual kitchen facilities. But a meal for a big crowd puts special demands on almost any house, host, and hostess. I am not mad about buffet dining, but when it is unavoidable I like guests to help themselves to the main course, then be served more wine and second helpings. I like their plates to be cleared and the dessert to be passed to them.

In this menu, the oyster bar makes for fun and informality, but it does need a special place of its own. After serving them, arrange with a good friend, or your helper if you have one, to dismantle the remains of the once splendid setup while the guests are moving on to the main course. At home, Paul and I have enough room so we can enjoy our oysters in one place and then grandly waft everyone off to another for the sit-down part of dinner. We generally arrange platters at either end of our long table, so that people can help themselves quickly and find a place to sit down.

In any crowd, there are invariably a few people who simply cannot face oysters, so we offer them a simple alternative like cheese or thinly sliced salami. We allow three oysters per person, which seems to average out for those who can leave them and those who so love them that they will eat four or five or even more. Now that we have learned to open them easily, we do so as we serve them, which is always advisable anyway. Once our guests get the knack of prying up the shells with a beer can opener, or, as college wags used to put it, a church key, we find that most of them find it great fun doing their own. We set out plates and napkins, oyster forks for the conventionally minded, and spoons for those who eat oysters, as we do, in one voluptuous slurp. We add lemons and a pepper grinder—but no cocktail sauce!—and buttered dark bread.

The Turkey Orloff is a modern, streamlined cousin of an elaborate dish, Veal Prince Orloff, named for a notable Russian gourmet of the nineteenth century by some forgotten Paris chef. It is a saddle of veal that is roasted, sliced, then re-formed with a stuffing of mushrooms and *soubise* (rice braised with onions) and gratinéed with a rich creamy sauce. It is a noble dish; but its price is almost prohibitive since you must use a very choice cut of veal, and it is almost fiendishly fattening. The turkey variant is much less expensive, less rich—and less work. But it is a recipe designed for the food processor, where you can make light of slicing 15 cups of onions and mincing quarts of mushrooms. If fresh sliced turkey breast is not available at the supermarket, frozen breasts always are. The finished dish, whose layers of white turkey meat are interleaved with a rice, onion, and mushroom stuffing and finished off with a golden gratin, has a deep, subtle flavor and an agreeable, fork-tender texture.

When you're planning a vegetable here, you have to think about the number of people you're serving, and about your kitchen facilities. A great platter of hot broccoli, fresh peas, or beans would be lovely. But for 19 people? That's much too difficult, I think. I'd rather have something cold, but not the usual green salad. Instead, I have chosen a beautiful platter of fresh green beans, cooked, chilled, and lightly dressed with oil, lemon, and mustard, and brightened up with red onion rings and tomatoes.

Dessert for a crowd. You want it dressy, delectable, original, but easy to handle. The idea here is simple indeed: storebought vanilla ice cream, each serving topped with a spoonful or two of dark rum, then dusted with powdered coffee. It's a surprise dessert with a sophisticated air—and there's something wonderfully sensuous about spooning up this ambrosial combination from a big opulent goblet that a pedestrian old bowl simply doesn't supply.

Preparations

Recommended Equipment:
For your oyster bar, you will need a space about the size of two card tables, a big tub and plenty of chopped ice for the oysters, some kind of receptacle for their shells, a pepper mill or two, and several beer can openers. Have paring knives for separating the muscles from the shells and a conventional oyster knife or two for recalcitrant cases.

For every multiple of the turkey recipe (which is given for 8 persons), you'll want a baking-and-serving dish 2 inches (5 cm) deep. As I've said, the turkey recipe is designed for the food processor; if you don't have one, see suggestions for other main courses in Menu Variations.

Marketing and Storage:

A note on quantities: the recipes, and therefore the lists below, are for 8 "average" appetites. Multiply by 2½ if the dinner is for 19—or even 20—people.

Staples to have on hand

Salt
Peppercorns
Mustard (the strong Dijon type)
Herbs: dried tarragon, thyme or sage, imported bay leaves
Flour
Celery, onions, and carrots (small quantities for making stock)

Garlic
Powdered instant coffee (for the dessert topping)

Specific ingredients for this menu

Turkey breast (either 2½ pounds or 1¼ kg fresh slices or half a frozen 9-pound or 4-kg bone-in breast) ▼
Fresh oysters in the shell (24 to 30)
Salami (16 thin slices)
Cheese (if you wish it, as an alternative to oysters)
Cocktail sausages (16)
Olive oil or salad oil (4 ounces or 1 dL)
Plain raw white rice (2 ounces or 60 g or ¼ cup)
Thin-sliced dark bread (20 slices), pumpernickel or rye
French bread, 2 loaves
Butter (½ pound or 225 g or 2 sticks)
Eggs (3)
Low-fat cottage cheese (4 ounces or 115 g)
Mozzarella cheese (4 ounces or 115 g), coarsely grated
Fresh mushrooms (½ pound or 225 g)
Yellow onions (1 pound or 450 g, or 5 or 6 medium-size)
Red onions (2 medium-size) or scallions (1 bunch)
Cherry tomatoes (1 quart or 1 L) or ripe red regular tomatoes (3 or 4)
Watercress (2 or 3 bunches) or romaine (1 head)
Fresh green beans (2½ pounds or 1¼ kg)
Fresh parsley
Lemons (5)
Vanilla ice cream (1½ quarts or 1½ L), best quality
Dark Jamaica rum (8 ounces or ½ L)
Crushed ice for the oysters and ice cubes for drinks

▶ *Remarks:*

In providing for non-oyster-eaters with cheese, salami slices, and hot cocktail sausages, I allow about 2 ounces of each per person, since some oyster eaters will consume both. I also count on 2 or 3 slices of dark bread per person, and 2 tablespoons softened butter to spread on each 10 to 12 pieces. *Turkey breast:* Fresh ready-sliced turkey breast meat is available in many markets: look in the poultry section, where it is usually attractively packaged in flat see-through trays. If you are buying frozen breasts, the best size, I think, is around 9 pounds (4 kg); have the breast sawed in half lengthwise if you are doing the turkey recipe for only 8 people, and you can store the other half in your freezer. It is always best to defrost frozen turkey slowly in the refrigerator, since you will then have juicier and firmer meat.

Turkey Talk:

You can begin with sliced raw fresh turkey breast meat, or with half a 9-pound (4-kg) frozen turkey breast. Once a turkey breast has thawed, peel off and discard the skin, remove the breast meat in one piece from the bone, and cut it into 12 or more serving slices about ⅜ inch (1 cm) thick with a very sharp knife.

The Stock:

Chop up the carcass and simmer it and any turkey meat scraps for 2 hours in lightly salted water to cover, with a chopped carrot and onion, 2 celery ribs, and an herb bouquet (8 parsley sprigs, 1 large imported bay leaf, and ½ teaspoon thyme or sage tied in washed cheesecloth); strain, degrease, and refrigerate until needed.

If you've no homemade stock, use canned chicken broth but flavor it as follows: for each 2 cups (½ L), simmer for 30 minutes with 3 tablespoons each sliced onions, carrots, and celery, ½ cup (1 dL) dry white wine *or* ⅓ cup (¾ dL) dry white French vermouth; then strain.

Turkey Orloff

Turkey breast scallopini gratinéed with mushrooms, onions, rice, and cheese

For 8 people

¼ cup (½ dL) plain raw white rice
Salt
1 pound (450 g or 5 to 6 medium-size) onions
1½ sticks (6 ounces or 180 g) butter
1 egg plus 2 egg yolks
½ pound (225 g or 3 to 3½ cups) fresh mushrooms
A handful fresh parsley sprigs (to make 3 Tb minced)
½ tsp fragrant dried tarragon
Pepper
12 or more turkey breast slices (see notes preceding recipe)
5 Tb flour for sauce, plus extra for turkey sauté
1 Tb vegetable oil
3 cups (¾ L) hot turkey stock (or chicken stock—see notes preceding recipe)
½ cup (1 dL) low-fat cottage cheese
1 cup (¼ L or 4 ounces) lightly pressed down coarsely grated mozzarella cheese

Rice and onion soubise

Preheat oven to 325°F/170°C. Drop the rice into a saucepan with 2 quarts (2 L) rapidly boiling salted water and boil uncovered for exactly 5 minutes; drain immediately and

reserve. Meanwhile peel and then chop the onions in a food processor (it needs no washing until after its last operation). To do onions, prechop roughly by hand into 1-inch (2½-cm) chunks and process them 1½ cups (3½ dL) at a time, using metal blade and switching machine on and off 3 or 4 times at 1-second intervals to chop onions into ⅜-inch (1-cm) morsels. Melt 4 tablespoons of the butter in a flameproof 6- to 8-cup (1½- to 2-L) baking dish, stir in the chopped onions, the drained rice, and ¼ teaspoon salt, mixing well to coat with the butter; cover the dish and bake in middle level of oven for about 1 hour, stirring up once or twice, until rice is completely tender and beginning to turn a golden yellow. When the rice is done and still warm, beat in the egg; taste carefully and correct seasoning.

🕐 May be done a day or two in advance.

Mushroom duxelles

While rice and onion *soubise* is cooking, trim and wash the mushrooms. For the food processor, first chop roughly by hand into 1-inch (2½-cm) chunks, then process into ⅛-inch (½-cm) pieces, using the 1-second on-off technique. Mince the parsley in the machine afterward. By handfuls, either twist mushrooms hard in the corner of a towel or squeeze through a potato ricer to extract as much of their juices as possible. Sauté the mushrooms in 2 tablespoons of the butter in a medium-size frying pan over moderately high heat, stirring and tossing until mushroom pieces begin to separate from each other—5 to 6 minutes. Stir in the tarragon and parsley; season to taste with salt and pepper. Stir half of the mixture into the cooked rice and onion *soubise;* reserve the rest.

🕐 Mushroom *duxelles* may be cooked in advance and may be frozen.

Preparing the turkey scallopini

Pound the slices between 2 sheets of wax paper, with a rubber hammer, a rolling pin, or the side of a bottle, to expand them about double and to thin them down by half. These are your turkey scallopini; cover and refrigerate them until you are ready to sauté them.

Sautéing the turkey scallopini

Salt and pepper the turkey slices lightly, dredge in flour and shake off excess, sauté for about a minute on each side in the oil and 2 tablespoons of the butter (more if needed) — just to stiffen them and barely cook through. Set slices aside on a plate as you finish them.

The gratinéing sauce

Make a turkey *velouté* sauce as follows. Melt 4 tablespoons of the butter over moderate heat in a heavy-bottomed 2-quart (2-L) saucepan, blend in the flour, and cook, stirring with a wooden spoon, until flour and butter foam and froth together for 2 minutes without turning more than a golden yellow. Remove from heat and, when this *roux* has stopped bubbling, pour in 2 cups (½ L) of the hot turkey or chicken stock and blend vigorously with a wire whip. Return to heat, stirring slowly with wire whip to reach all over bottom, corner, and side of pan, and boil slowly for 2 minutes. Taste and correct seasoning. Sauce should be thick enough to coat a wooden spoon nicely, mean-

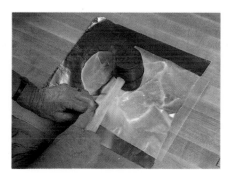

ing it will coat the turkey. Beat in more stock by droplets if sauce is too thick. In the food processor or an electric blender, purée the egg yolks with the cottage cheese (or push through a fine sieve and beat in a bowl with a wire whip); by dribbles, beat the hot sauce into the egg yolk and cheese mixture.

Assembling the dish

Choose a baking-and-serving dish about 10 by 14 by 2 inches (25 x 35 x 5 cm); butter the inside, and spread a thin layer of sauce in bottom of dish. Make a neat, slightly overlapping pattern of the turkey slices down the center of the dish, spreading each, as you go, with the *soubise.* Spoon remaining mushroom *duxelles* down the sides. Spoon remaining sauce over the turkey and spread the mozzarella cheese on top.

🕐   Recipe may be prepared a day in advance to this point; when cool, cover and refrigerate. If, before proceeding, you note that the sauce does not cover some parts of the meat, spread more mozzarella on these areas.

Final baking and serving

Turkey will take about 25 minutes to heat and for the top to brown; it should be served fairly promptly since the meat will be juicier if it does not have to wait around. Set uncovered in upper third of a preheated 400°F/200°C oven until contents are bubbling hot and sauce has browned nicely.

Fresh Green Beans with Watercress and Tomatoes, Oil and Lemon Dressing

For 8 people
2½ pounds (1¼ kg) fresh green beans, trimmed and blanched
Salt and pepper
2 or 3 bunches watercress, or 1 head romaine
For the dressing
1 lemon
1 small clove garlic (optional)
1 tsp prepared mustard, Dijon type
6 or more Tb olive oil or salad oil
2 medium-size mild red onions, or 1 bunch scallions
1 quart (1 L) cherry tomatoes, or 3 or 4 ripe red regular tomatoes

Prepare the beans in the morning, wrap in a clean towel and then in a plastic bag, and refrigerate. Also remove tough stems from watercress, wash the cress, and fold in a clean towel and plastic; refrigerate (or, if using romaine, wash, separating leaves, wrap like the cress, and refrigerate).

An hour or so before serving, prepare the dressing as follows. Cut the zest (yellow part of

peel) off half the lemon and mince very fine. Place in a small mortar or heavy bowl with the salt; purée in the optional garlic. Pound into a fine paste with a pestle or the end of a wooden spoon, then beat in the mustard, a tablespoon of juice from the lemon, and the oil. Carefully correct seasoning—dressing should not be too acid, only mildly so, because of the wine you will be serving with the dinner.

Peel the red onions and slice into thin rings; toss in a bowl with the dressing (or mix chopped scallions with the dressing); cover and refrigerate. Halve the cherry tomatoes, place cut side up in a dish, and salt lightly (or peel, slice, and lightly salt regular tomatoes); cover and refrigerate. If you are using romaine rather than cress, gather leaves by handfuls and slice crosswise into ⅜-inch (1-cm) julienne strips; refrigerate in a plastic bag.

Shortly before guests are to arrive, arrange the watercress or romaine in the bottom of a wide salad bowl or platter and toss with a sprinkling of salt. Toss the blanched beans in a bowl with the onions or scallions and dressing, taste carefully for seasoning, and arrange attractively over the cress or romaine, with the tomatoes around the edges. Baste tomatoes and beans with dressing left in bean bowl. Cover and keep cool until serving time.

Jamaican Ice Cream Goblet

This dessert needs no actual recipe since it consists only of a healthy helping of the best vanilla ice cream in a big goblet (if possible! or a pretty bowl or a dessert plate), a spoonful or two of dark Jamaica rum, and a sprinkling of powdered instant coffee (if you have only the freeze-dried granular type, pulverize it in a blender). It couldn't be simpler, but the rum and coffee blending into that vanilla cream combine into a marvelous medley of tastes. I usually assemble this in the kitchen, with a friend or two to help pass it around. But with not too big a crowd, it's rather fun to pass the goblets of ice cream and let guests help themselves to the rum, in a pitcher with ladle, and to the coffee, in a bowl with teaspoon.

P.S. Bourbon whiskey can substitute for rum—but in that case it must be called a Bourbon rather than a Jamaican goblet.

🕐 Timing

Midway through your menu, perhaps when you move on from the oysters to the turkey, remember to take your ice cream out of the freezer and put it into the refrigerator to soften.

Just before the guests arrive, assemble the salad platters while you heat the cocktail sausages or crisp the French bread.

Since Turkey Orloff shouldn't sit around too much after its 25- to 30-minute baking, when you put it in depends on your party-giving style.

An hour or so before the guests are to arrive, slice the onions, tomatoes, and other green bean fixings. Set up the oyster bar.

In the morning, blanch and chill the beans, wash and pick over the cress or wash the romaine. Butter the brown bread for the oysters, etc.; stack the slices on a tray between sheets of wax paper and chill, ready to be arranged on a board or platter when you set up the oyster bar. Buy the ice.

You can assemble the Turkey Orloff in the morning or the day before, and as you'll see from the recipe, parts of it may be made days in advance.

A day or even two or three before the party, buy the oysters, clean them, and stack them.

Buy the wines and other drinkables well ahead, so that those needing remedial rest will have their due.

Menu Variations

Oysters: You could also include clams and cooked shrimp. For a quite different dish—but similar in also being something raw, not too highly flavored, and obviously very special—serve Steak Tartare. Grind it yourself from beef tenderloin butts or tails, season lightly with salt and pepper, beat in raw egg yolks (one per half pound), and serve the trimmings separately: more salt, a pepper grinder or two, capers, anchovy fillets, finely minced onion, and chopped fresh herbs like parsley and chives. Guests pile their own on buttered dark bread and mix in the trimmings of their choice.

Turkey Orloff: For other dishes comprising poultry with an elegant stuffing, you might consider a boned stuffed turkey *ballottine* (as described in *The French Chef Cookbook*), or Chicken Melon (see *Julia's Breakfasts, Lunches, and Suppers*, page 22) served hot, or boned ducks or chickens in pastry crusts. You could make your Orloff dish with chicken, veal, or thinly sliced loin of pork.

Vegetable or salad: Delicious, in season, would be fresh asparagus vinaigrette, or artichoke hearts with a few halved cherry tomatoes for decorations. A platter of sliced cucumbers with a light dressing and a wreath of watercress is another green idea, or that always amenable standby, fresh broccoli vinaigrette. Finally, just have fine big bowls of fresh mixed salad greens.

Dessert: You could make peach Melba, or serve your ice cream with poached pears and chocolate sauce (*poires belle Hélène*), or garnish the ice cream with canned peaches simmered in their own syrup that has been boiled down with wine and cinnamon. And there are a thousand ways of using liqueurs, of freezing store ice cream into a bombe, and of serving it with meringues. Or change from ice cream to fruit and have a macédoine; and with it you could serve cake or cookies.

Leftovers

Turkey Orloff: You can reassemble, sprinkle on more cheese, and regratiné the dish; it will not have quite its original glory, but it will still make very good eating. You can chop the turkey bits, mix everything together, and use for stuffing crêpes; or make an elegant turkey hash. Or grind everything up in a food processor, add a little fresh sausage meat, and 1 egg per cup of mixture, and turn it into a meat loaf. Or chop or grind up everything and simmer with a chicken stock to make a rich and hearty soup.

Green beans: I would prefer not to have leftovers in this category since the beauty of the fresh bean is fleeting. Serve them again the very next day as a salad would be my suggestion. However, you could try dropping the whole mixture briefly in boiling water to wash off the dressing, draining, and boiling up in a soup.

Postscript

Luxury and quantity, like the lion and the lamb, don't often consort; and it is not easy to serve a really fine meal to great numbers, especially without expert household help. I won't bore you with admonitions about counting silver, shifting furniture, and all those preparatory chores; but it is very certain that planning is the essence of a successful party, and I do think too many hosts skimp on menu planning, though this is the most important thing of all. My own practice is to choose a simple workable menu and to do as much as possible in advance, such as freezing what can be frozen of the menu's elements, like the *duxelles,* precooking the stock and *soubise* for the turkey, and saving a bit of that valuable last-minute time for some truly special touch. Nothing gives a party so much personal warmth as the guests' sense that you wanted to give them a particular treat. One remarkable dish has twice the effect of several run-of-the-mill ones.

At this intimate dinner you can cook right at the table and not miss a word of the conversation. And for chocolate lovers, there is a treat in store.

Chafing-Dish Dinner

Menu

Seviche of Sea Scallops with Fresh Artichokes

Steak Diane
Fresh Green Peas
Real Mashed Potatoes

Le Gâteau Victoire au Chocolat, Mousseline

Suggested wines:
Alsatian Riesling, Chablis, or Muscadet with the seviche; a Cabernet or red Bordeaux with the steak. With the cake (optional), a Champagne, a sparkling Vouvray, or a Sauternes

What to do about conversations you can't bear to miss? Cook at the table, of course, says Paul, adding sagely that we'd better practice first. How right he is. Chafing-dish jokes, featuring splashes and scorches, were a staple in our parents' day, when the kitchen belonged exclusively to the cook but the family tried to play too. People nowadays do seem to use chafing dishes on buffet tables, as food warmers, but are apt to ignore their usefulness as small, real stoves, not to mention their dramatic possibilities.

Flambé dishes are fun but a bit too obviously showy. So we settle on Steak Diane, to make a party chic as well as intimate. Why Diane? Nobody remembers. Why a French name, since it's not related to the French Sauce Diane, a creamed-up version of the classic gamy *poivrade?* Anne Willan, in her Grand Diplôme series, suggests that the dish originated in Australia. Anyway, that touch of Worcestershire sauce would indicate the New World—but if the dish resembles its namesake, the mysterious Diane must have been quite a girl: good-looking, classy, brisk, and modish but not faddy. The sauce has a tangy, refreshing taste, not too overpowering before a rich dessert. The meat is pounded to make it thinner for swift searing; and for this you need a very strong heat source (see Recommended Equipment for details). We have experimented with various fuels and have found that liquid denatured alcohol is an absolute essential because of its hot, clear, odorless flame. For Steak Diane we practice such flourishes as pouring oil from on high, and turning the meat with a deft flick of the wrist—two wrists, I mean, one for each fork. Great fun.

If you have friends who are chocolate addicts, do something special to indulge their passion. For instance, there used to be a chocolate cake in New York in the thirties, legendary among connoisseurs. It was made by a smart little bakery whose dour proprietress has never revealed her secret recipe. This much-discussed cake, which I unfortunately never tasted in those halcyon days, was baked in a loaf shape and had a fat and unctuous texture and intense chocolate flavor; it sank in the middle, and this trough was, accordingly, mounded with curled shaved chocolate. Fanciers were all agreed that the cake must have involved a lot of butter, egg whites and yolks beaten separately, and practically no flour (one very skillful cook, it was said, evolved a near replica using only one tablespoonful). But what effect, I wonder, would so little flour have, anyway? I made a number of serious tries, but then sailed off on a different tack. What finally came out of endless experiments was a cake I have proudly named Le Gâteau Victoire au Chocolat, Mousseline. Its components sound like custard makings, its airiness suggests a mousse, and yet, it is a cake: a cake with no butter, no flour at all, a simple

method, and an incredibly sparse list of ingredients. Sparse but sumptuous: it includes one whole pound of chocolate.

I happen to love the old-fashioned combination of peas and mashed potatoes—plain but exquisite if you have good fresh peas and Idaho potatoes, and wonderful with steak. You might think this would involve long minutes away from the table. But mashed potatoes can, in fact, be done ahead and kept warm: the trick is to cover them only partially, to give them air. (By that same token, a baked potato also acquires a dank, stifled flavor if you let it sit unopened. Slash it and give it a squeeze.) By doctoring them with cheese and whatnot, busy people can make do pretty well with dehydrated or otherwise pre-prepared potatoes; but these are not for plain mashing. You must use the real thing. Why not recoup peeling time by shelling the peas mechanically? I have found an ingenious device, something like an old-fashioned laundry mangle in miniature, which you can crank by hand or else attach to an ordinary electric beater (see page 34). You feed the pea pods into it and, with efficient little zips, it gobbles up the pods and spews them out one side while the peas—quite unharmed—bounce briskly out the other. This chapter's section on Menu Variations does not include vegetables, since almost all vegetables are good with steak; but my recommendation, if the menu seems too starchy to you, would be to substitute tomatoes, baked or *à la provençale* (with garlic, olive oil, and bread crumbs), and string beans or broccoli for the peas and mashed potatoes.

Anyway, the goloptiousness, as Winnie-the-Pooh would have said, of this menu decided us on a light first course—rather reminiscent of the *nouvelle cuisine*—which has a good deal of subtle charm. Sea scallops are sliced into a lime juice marinade which "cooks" them briefly—something to do with enzymes, I understand. Then they are arranged with sliced fresh artichoke bottoms, tomatoes, and watercress or romaine; the delicate sauce *vinaigrette* is given a little body by the addition of an egg white.

With its easy, uninterrupted flow, this kind of little dinner is usually a happy one. My own enthusiasm is divided about equally among the nimble pea sheller, the efficient, energy-saving little stove, and that super chocolate cake.

Preparations

Recommended Equipment:
For the potatoes and the peas, you'll need a potato ricer and two heavy pots. For the cake, a 10-cup (2½-L) cake pan, which must be at least 2 inches (5 cm) deep. I usually measure a new pan's capacity by pouring it full of water and measuring the amount; then I scratch "10 c" or whatever on the back of the pan. A nonstick surface is strongly recommended. You need a larger pan, also, to serve as a bain-marie (water bath) for the cake pan.

For your dinner table: see the Steak Diane recipe for the sauce setup, which should be conveniently arranged on a tray. You'll need an electric warming tray, or trays, with room

enough for dinner plates, a small serving dish for the steaks, and a serving dish or dishes for the vegetables. The heat source should sit on a metal tray. You can use an electric skillet or a camp stove in place of a chafing dish; all you need for tabletop sautéing is strong heat and a wide pan. About chafing dishes: many pretty ones of open, leggy design, while fine for scrambling eggs or other slow-heat cookery, don't work for sautéing. This is because you need a focused flame, which you can't get unless it is enclosed at the sides with just enough air circulation to keep it burning. You could surround a leggy chafing dish with a collar of sheet metal with a few holes cut in near the top. Denatured alcohol gel won't give you enough heat; you must have liquid denatured alcohol.

And play safe: if you have to replenish the fuel (though the usual-sized container will hold enough for hours), douse the flame and let the lamp cool a bit before adding more alcohol. And in the—very unlikely—case of fire, have baking soda handy and remember that the quickest way to extinguish any blazing pan is to clap a well-fitting lid on it.

For serving your cake you will need a platter or board with flat surface large enough to hold the unmolded cake.

Marketing and Storage:
Staples to have on hand

Salt
Black and white peppercorns
Optional: bottled green peppercorns ▼
Mustard (the strong Dijon type)
Soy sauce
Worcestershire sauce
Olive oil
Optional: peanut oil
Flour
Cornstarch
Unsweetened baking chocolate (2 ounces or 60 g)

Semisweet baking chocolate (14 ounces or 400 g)
Sugar (about ½ cup or 1 dL)
Optional: confectioners sugar
Pure vanilla extract
Eggs (7 "large")
Butter
Heavy or whipping cream (at least 2 cups or ½ L)
Milk
"Baking" potatoes (3 or 4 large) ▼
Parsley
Shallots or scallions
Limes (1)
Lemons (3 or 4)
Beef bouillon (1 cup or ¼ L)
Instant coffee
Cognac
Port or Madeira
Dark Jamaica rum

Specific ingredients for this menu

Steaks (4; see recipe)
Fresh sea scallops (8 to 10 large)
Artichokes (2 or 3 large fine)
Fresh green peas (about 2 pounds or 1 kg) ▼
Watercress or romaine
Tomatoes (2 or 3) or cherry tomatoes

▶ ## Remarks:
Staples

Green peppercorns: buy them "au naturel," meaning they are packed in lightly salted water. They will keep several weeks in the refrigerator; for longer storage freeze them.
Potatoes for mashing: you want floury potatoes so that they mash fluffily; you don't want new potatoes or waxy potatoes, which mash lumpily, and even glue-ily.

Ingredients for this menu

Storebought fresh *peas* can be perfectly good, although not always as fresh and as young as you would like. But properly cooked, they're so much better than frozen or canned. Be sure the pods are fresh and crisp and neither too full (meaning the peas are large and old) nor too flat (meaning the peas have not formed). If in doubt, discreetly tear open the package a little bit and taste—right there in the supermarket.

Seviche of Sea Scallops with Fresh Artichokes

Sea scallops have a lovely freshness of taste and texture when sliced thin and marinated raw in lime juice, salt, parsley, and minced shallots or scallions—the lime juice cooks them, as it were. For a light first course you need only 2 or 3 per serving, and half a large artichoke bottom plus a little fresh tomato and watercress or romaine for decoration.

For 4 servings

8 to 10 large fresh sea scallops
1 fresh lime
Salt and white pepper
½ Tb minced shallots or scallions
2 Tb minced fresh parsley
2 Tb flour
2 or 3 lemons
2 or 3 large fine artichokes
1 tsp Dijon-type mustard
1 Tb raw egg white
4 to 5 Tb light olive oil
For decoration: watercress or shredded romaine, sliced tomatoes or cherry tomatoes

The scallops

Wash and drain the scallops to remove possible sand. Dipping a sharp knife in cold water for each cut, slice them crosswise (across the grain) into pieces 3/16 inch (¾ cm) thick.

Toss in a bowl with the juice of the lime, a sprinkling of salt and pepper, the shallots or scallions, and the parsley. Cover and marinate (let sit) in the refrigerator for half an hour, or until serving time.

The artichokes

To make a *blanc* or cooking liquid that will keep the artichokes white, place the flour in a medium-size saucepan, gradually beat in 1 cup (¼ L) cold water, stir in 2 more cups (½ L) water, a tablespoon of lemon juice, and 1½ teaspoons salt; bring to the boil, stirring, then remove from heat. One by one, break stems off artichokes and bend leaves back upon themselves all around to snap them off the base until you come to the bulge at the top of the artichoke bottom; cut off crown of leaves at this point, and trim base all around to remove greenish parts—rubbing frequently with cut lemon to prevent darkening. Drop each as done into the cooking water. Simmer 30 to 40 minutes, until tender when pierced with a knife, and leave in cooking water until ready to serve.

🕐 Will keep 2 to 3 days under refrigeration.

Wash under cold water, scoop out chokes with a teaspoon, and cut into 3/16-inch (¾ cm) slices going from top to bottom. Fold gently in a bowl with the following dressing.

Vinaigrette Liée:

(lightly thickened French dressing)
For about ⅓ cup dressing, beat ½ teaspoon salt with 1½ tablespoons lemon juice and the teaspoon of mustard, beat in the egg white, and then, by dribbles, the oil. Taste carefully for seasoning, adding pepper to taste—dressing should not be too strong or it will mask the taste of the artichokes.

Assembling

Line individual small plates or shells with watercress or shredded romaine. Then arrange slices of artichoke interspersed with tomato, for instance, around the edges of the dishes and a rosette of scallop slices in the middle, with a central dot of tomato for accent. Cover with plastic wrap and refrigerate until serving time.

🕐 May be prepared up to an hour ahead.

Steak Diane

For 4 people

4 steaks (about ½ pound or 225 g trimmed) cut ½ inch (1½ cm) thick from the top loin strip (or tenderloin, or Delmonico, or rib-eye steaks)

1½ Tb green peppercorns packed in water, or freshly ground pepper

Drops of soy sauce

Olive oil or peanut oil

The Sauce Setup for the Dining Room:

A small pitcher of oil and a plate with a stick of butter

¼ cup (½ dL) each minced shallots or scallions and fresh parsley, in small bowls

A pitcher or bowl containing 1 Tb cornstarch blended with 1 Tb Dijon mustard and 1 cup fragrant beef bouillon

Worcestershire sauce

A lemon cut in half

Cognac and Port or Madeira

Equipment

A heavy frying pan about 12 inches (30 cm) top diameter for tabletop sautéing; a strong heat source; 2 large forks for turning and rolling up steaks; 2 dessert spoons, 1 for stirring and 1 for tasting; a butter knife; matches; 4 hot dinner plates

Preliminaries

Trim steaks of all fat and gristle—especially the piece of gristle at large end of loin under fat. One at a time, pound steaks between pieces of wax paper to enlarge them and reduce them to an even ¼-inch (¾-cm) thickness; use a wooden mallet, metal pounder, rubber hammer, rolling pin, bottle, or other handy object. Crush drained green peppercorns with the back of a spoon and spread a little on one side of each steak (or rub into steaks a grind or two of regular pepper) along with a few drops soy sauce and oil. Roll up each steak like a rug from one of the small ends and arrange on a platter; cover and refrigerate until serving time.

Prepare ingredients for the sauce setup.
🕐   May be done several hours in advance. Cover shallots or scallions and parsley with dampened paper towels and plastic wrap and refrigerate; refrigerate the bouillon mixture.

Sautéing Steaks Diane at the table

Preheat frying pan in the kitchen to a reasonably hot temperature and bring it and the steaks with you to the table. The sauce setup should be already in place near the chafing-dish burner.

The steaks are sautéed two at a time as follows: pour 1 tablespoon oil into the pan as it heats on the flame and add 2 tablespoons butter. Butter will foam up, gradually foam will subside, and just as butter begins to brown, unroll one steak and immediately a second in the pan. Sauté 30 to 40 seconds on one side, turn with forks, and sauté on the other side—steaks will barely color and will just become lightly springy to the touch—for rare. Rapidly roll them up with your forks and replace on the platter. Sauté the other two steaks in the same manner, and roll up beside the first.

Add another spoonful or two butter, and when foaming stir in a big spoonful of shallots or scallions and parsley, let cook for a moment, then stir in the pitcher or bowl of bouillon mixture. Stir about for a moment, then add a few drops of Worcestershire and the juice of half a lemon (pierce lemon with fork, picking out seeds first, and squeeze with flourish). Add droplets of Cognac and Port or Madeira, taste, and add droplets more—again with flourish. Finally, with forks and fanfare, and one by one, unroll each steak and bathe in the sauce, turning and dipping with your two forks, before placing it on a hot dinner plate.

When the other steaks are sauced and in place, spoon the rest of the sauce over them and serve.

Fresh Green Peas

(the storebought kind)

For 4 people

3 cups (¾ L) shelled fresh peas (about 2
pounds or 1 kg large fresh peas in the shell)

Salt

2 or more Tb butter

1 or more tsp sugar

Pepper

2 Tb minced scallions (optional)

Drop the peas into a large saucepan containing
at least 3 quarts (3 liters) rapidly boiling salted
water and boil slowly, uncovered, for 5 minutes or more, until just cooked through—taste
several to make sure. Immediately drain and
refresh for several minutes in cold water to set
the green color and preserve the fresh texture.

🕐 May be precooked several hours in
advance; cover and refrigerate.

Half an hour or so before serving, smear
a heavy saucepan with butter, pour in the
peas, and toss with 1 teaspoon sugar. Several
minutes before serving, toss with salt, pepper,
and the optional scallions and add several
tablespoons water. Cover and bring to the
rapid boil, tossing, to warm through. Taste
carefully for seasoning—you may wish a little
more sugar, just enough to give the illusion of
fresh-picked sweetness. Toss with more butter
if you like, turn into a hot dish, and serve
immediately.

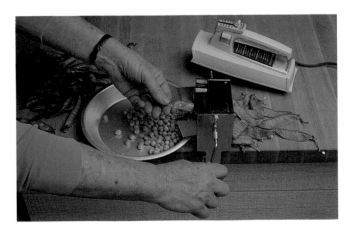

Real Mashed Potatoes

For 4 people

3 or 4 large "baking" potatoes

Salt

Milk and/or cream

Butter

White pepper

    Equipment

A potato ricer

Wash and peel the potatoes, cut into lengthwise quarters, and set in a saucepan with
lightly salted water to cover. Boil for 15 minutes or so, until potatoes are tender when
pierced with a knife—cut a piece in half and
taste to be sure. Immediately drain and put
through ricer into a heavy-bottomed saucepan.
Stir with a wooden spoon over moderate heat
for a minute or more until potatoes begin to
film bottom of pan, indicating excess moisture
has been evaporated. Beat in several tablespoons milk and/or cream to lighten them
slightly, then a tablespoon butter, and salt and
white pepper to taste. If you are serving immediately, beat in milk and/or cream until the
potatoes are the consistency you wish, and
more butter if you like, then turn into a hot
dish and serve at once.

🕐 You may cook them an hour or so ahead.
In this case, add only a minimum of milk
and/or cream and butter and set pan of potatoes in another and larger pan of hot but not
simmering water. Cover the potato pan only
partially—hot potatoes must not be covered
airtight or they develop an off taste. At serving
time, uncover, raise heat, and beat the potatoes
with a wooden spoon, beating in more milk
and/or cream and butter to taste.

Le Gâteau Victoire au Chocolat, Mousseline

Chocolate mousse dessert cake

Here is a very tender, moist, and delicate, and very chocolaty, dessert confection that is more like a cheesecake or custard than a cake, yet it is a cake—almost. However, it is cooked in a bain-marie—a pan of barely simmering water —in the oven, and it contains no flour or starch and no baking powder, only chocolate, a little sugar, eggs, and whipped cream. It is best served tepid, or at least at room temperature.

For a 10-cup (2½-L) cake pan, such as a square one 9 by 9 by 2 inches (23 x 23 x 5 cm), serving 8 to 10 or more

1 Tb instant coffee
4 Tb hot water
4 Tb dark Jamaica rum
14 ounces (400 g) semisweet baking chocolate
2 ounces (60 g) unsweetened baking chocolate
6 "large" eggs
½ cup (100 g) sugar
1 cup (¼ L) heavy or whipping cream, chilled
1 Tb pure vanilla extract
Confectioners sugar
Equipment
A 10-cup (2½-L) cake pan, preferably with nonstick lining, buttered, bottom lined with buttered wax paper, and floured; an electric mixer with round-bottomed bowl or a hand-held mixer or a large whisk and a metal bowl of the same type

Preliminaries

Preheat oven to 350°F/180°C and place rack in lower third level. Prepare cake pan. Choose a roasting pan large enough to hold cake pan easily, fill with enough hot water to come half-way up cake pan, and set in oven. Assemble all ingredients and equipment.

The chocolate

Swirl the coffee and hot water in a medium-size saucepan, add the rum, and break up the chocolate into the pan. Bring 2 inches (5 cm) of water to the boil in a larger pan, remove from heat, and set chocolate pan in it; cover and let the chocolate melt while you continue with the recipe.

The egg and sugar mixture

Break the eggs into the beating bowl, add the sugar, and stir over hot water for several minutes until eggs are slightly warm to your finger—this makes beating faster and increases volume. Then beat for 5 minutes or more, until mixture has at least tripled in volume and forms a thick ribbon when a bit is lifted and falls from the beater; the eggs should be the consistency of lightly whipped cream. (You must have beating equipment that will keep the whole mass of egg moving at once, meaning a narrow rounded bowl and a beater that circulates about it continually.)

The whipped cream

Pour cream into a metal mixing bowl. Empty a tray of ice cubes into a larger bowl, cover them with cold water, then set the cream bowl into the larger ice-filled bowl. Beat with a hand-held mixer or large balloon whisk, using an up-and-down circular motion to whip in as much air as possible, until cream has doubled in volume and holds its shape softly. Whip in the vanilla.

Assembling and baking

Beat up the melted chocolate with a whisk; it should be smooth and silky. Scrape it into the egg-sugar mixture, blending rapidly with a rubber spatula, and when partially incorporated, fold in the whipped cream, deflating cream and eggs as little as possible. Turn batter into prepared cake pan, which will be about two-thirds filled. Set it at once in the pan of hot water in the preheated oven. Cake will rise

some ⅛ inch (½ cm) above edge of pan, and is done when a skewer or straw comes out clean—after about 1 hour of baking. Then turn off oven, leave oven door ajar, and let cake sit for 30 minutes in its pan of water, so that it will sink evenly. Remove from oven, still in its pan of water, and let sit for another 30 minutes so that it will firm up before unmolding and serving. Cake will sink down as it cools to about its original volume.

🕐 This cake is at its most tender and delicious when eaten slightly warm; however, you may cook it even a day or two in advance, leave it in its pan (covered when cool, and refrigerated), then set it in a 200°F/95°C oven for 20 minutes to warm gently.

Serving suggestions

Unmold the cake and decorate with a sprinkling of confectioners sugar, or with pipings of whipped cream, or with a soft chocolate icing (semisweet chocolate melted and beaten with a little soft butter). You may wish to pass a custard sauce or sweetened and vanilla-flavored whipped cream with the cake.

Remarks:

Since this is a most delicate confection with only enough body to hold itself together, it does not always cut neatly like a regular cake. Furthermore, once unmolded it cannot be lifted and transferred from one serving platter to another unless you reverse it again into its pan.

🕐 *Timing*

Coming into the dining room, your guests should feel like first nighters at a magic show. There, carefully disposed, are the props: dinner plates on their warming tray and an array of condiments and implements. Under the chafing dish, the alcohol lamp is ready for flaming: what next? But first, the appetizer. When this is eaten, there is a pause.

After removing the used plates to the kitchen, you start heating the steak pan on the stove, to speed things up in the dining room. You toss the blanched peas in their buttered pot and give a quick stir to the potatoes. In moments, you return with the vegetables to the dining room, set them on the warming tray, fetch the steaks and the hot pan, set it on the chafing dish, and begin. The actual job of making Steak Diane is a matter of 2 minutes in all for searing the steaks, which you do two at a time—it goes fast on such a hot, wide cooking surface—and then 2 minutes more for combining and reducing the sauce, and 1 minute for bathing the steaks in it. However, with your warming tray at hand, you have no reason to rush, and a suave performer never looks hurried.

In a second brief pause, you remove the dinner and serving dishes, and decorate the cake with the whipped cream you have standing ready (in the refrigerator in a sieve lined with cheesecloth, so it won't get watery while standing).

The cake can be made in the morning, or even the day before, but don't unmold it. Half an hour before dinner, warm it (if you wish) to tepid (see recipe), and unmold it just before you call in your guests.

In principle, the potatoes should be done as late as possible, but you'd be surprised how long they keep their goodness, partly uncovered over hot water.

All the appetizer elements can be prepared in the morning, for assembly not more than an hour before serving. You can blanch, drain, and chill the peas in the morning, and, that afternoon, set them in their buttered pot. During the day, pound the steaks and refrigerate till just before serving.

Well in advance and at leisure, carefully arrange your dinner table. For chafing-dish meals, I even make a check list, for an omission is almost as ignominious as forgetting the salt on a picnic!

Menu Variations

The appetizer: Before a hearty, tangy main course and a rich dessert, you want something light, like oysters or a little shellfish salad, or a piquant consommé. *Gravlaks* or smoked salmon would be appropriate in flavor and texture, but perhaps too simple-looking. Before dishes like steak and cake, it's nice to have something "composed."

The main course: The parameters, or ground rules, here are: something sautéed, with or without deglazing sauce; something not so redolent as to argue with dessert, and

Crêpes Suzette being bathed in orange butter and folded into a triangle before being flamed in Cognac and orange liqueur

something handsomely and quickly done. Many kinds of scallopini are practical; pounded steaks are a kind of scallopini anyway. Veal, chicken, turkey, pork tenderloin? And you can do these with the same Diane sauce. High heat is for delicate things. You could blanch and slice brains or sweetbreads beforehand, dredge with flour, and finish them at table with browned butter and capers; or dredge thinly sliced calf's liver and sauté, adding thin onion slices halfway through; or do chicken livers with sliced mushrooms. Shad roe is a chafing-dish classic, as are veal kidneys.

The vegetables: As noted earlier, anything goes with steak. What's good today in the market?

The dessert: I hate to commend any other cake to you until you have tried the Victoire. But if you want a chocolaty one with no last-minute worries, you might consider the almond-rich Reine de Saba ("Queen of Sheba") or Le Marquis, a chocolate sponge cake, both in *Mastering I,* or the all-chocolate layer cake, Le Glorieux, in *Mastering II,* where you will also find a chocolate-filled cake, La Charlotte Africaine, made with slices of yellow or white leftover cake. In *J.C.'s Kitchen,* there is a section on working with chocolate, and one remarkably light though buttery chocolate cake called L'Eminence Brune. This particular name is a small joke: on *l'éminence grise,* the "gray eminence," as Père Joseph du Tremblay, Cardinal Richelieu's secret counselor, was nicknamed in the seventeenth century—and also on the name of a certain beautiful, green-eyed Persian pussycat. Christening a cake in the fanciful French style is almost as much fun as creating it.

And then, of course, you might want to save your performance at the chafing dish for dessert. One thinks automatically of cherries jubilee (or ice cream with other hot, liqueur-flavored sauces, some of which are flamed), and of crêpes Suzette, or the many other dessert pancakes in *Mastering I* and in *J.C.'s Kitchen;* or you can make sweet omelets, stack them on a warm side dish, and create a sauce in the pan.

Leftovers

The smaller your party, the more precisely you can plan quantities; so, unless a guest can't make it at the last minute, you won't have much left over. If you should have one raw *steak,* for some such reason, you can put it to good use (and stretch it to feed two) in beef Stroganoff or in one of those pleasant Oriental dishes like sukiyaki or beef with pea pods. Or split it between the two of you next morning, in a good old steak-and-eggs.

Mashed potatoes, though, are worth making in an overlarge quantity for the sake of two nice by-products. In the proportion of 2 cups mashed potatoes to 3 egg yolks, beat the mixture smoothly to make *pommes duchesse,* which, piped through a large rosette tube, makes a handsome border for a platter or for ramekins. Or beat 1 egg yolk into 1 cup *warmed* mashed potatoes, beat in 1 table-spoonful each parsley and chives, and fold in 1 beaten egg white to make an excellent mixture for mashed-potato pancakes. If you have just a small amount of mashed potatoes left, use them to thicken a soup or add to a bread dough.

You could rewarm the *cake* to tepid (back in its mold, of course), or eat it cold and call it a mousse or a super-rich brownie.

Postscript: Cooking in public

Preparation is everything, as the length of this chapter's Timing section suggests. At our TV studio, we have a backstage kitchen, where we prepare our stand-in dishes and those which must emerge in finished form seconds after the star has been prepared before the cameras. Careful charts are made of the cooktop and working surfaces so that every implement and ingredient is on hand and in place. Bottle tops are unscrewed beforehand, wastebins—out of camera range--are strategically placed (everybody asks me, "When you fling scraps over your shoulder like that, where do they land?"), and shallots, scallions, tomatoes, etc., are chopped and measured beforehand. What I do for the cameras looks easy because it *is* easy, with all the dirty work out of the way. At home, it's not a cinch for anyone; and then the telephone rings just as the aspic jells or the soufflé gasps and sinks.

In private or public cooking, broad, firm gestures are the most efficient. Wallop your steaks! Whoosh up your egg whites! And, behind your chafing dish and before your guests, act with assurance and decisiveness. Let every move accomplish something, and don't twiddle. As brevity is the soul of wit, spareness or "line" is the basis of bravura. And "line" is a matter of practice and preparation, which really is not dirty work for those who love to cook.

Let it rain! This no-fuss, no-muss barbecue can be given indoors just as well.

Indoor/ Outdoor Barbecue

Menu

Buddha's Eye
Roast or Barbecued Butterflied Leg of Lamb
Homemade Pita Bread and Pita Pizzas
Topinambours (Jerusalem Artichokes)
A Mammoth Mixed Salad Garnished with
Feta Cheese, Dressed with Vinaigrette

❦

Zabaione Batardo Veneziano—Marsala-
flavored Bavarian cream

❦

Suggested wines:
Jugs or magnums of a hearty red, such as
Côtes du Rhône, Beaujolais, or Zinfandel

We love to eat out on a flowery terrace above a fragrant garden with a little breeze keeping everything astir; an occasional zesty whiff from the grill doesn't at all interfere with the roses and heliotrope. But in our part of the world there's an old saying, "If you don't like the weather, wait a minute," and, unfortunately, it works the other way too. Just as we have the coals ready, just as we take our grand big hunk of meat from its marinade, dark clouds herd up and cover the sun, a sudden evil wind flips the leaves inside out . . . and blam: here it comes, and in we go.

But all those good smells and sizzles, so appetizing in the open air, can be just a bit much inside with the windows shut against a downpour. By using a leg of lamb boned and flattened out, which can be grilled out of doors or roasted indoors with only a final browning under the broiler, we have solved the problem to our great satisfaction. And this method solves three other problems as well. Boning makes it possible to cook this big cut, whose flavor adapts so beautifully to marinating and grilling, over coals in a reasonable time, getting it cooked through without charring and without searing its odd shape unevenly. It makes carving a matter of seconds. And it produces glorious leftovers—which can't be said for shish kebab.

The heavy, complicated structure of tail, hip, and shank—almost half the weight of a lamb leg—is hard to carve around but easy to extract before cooking. If you've never boned meat before, a lamb leg would be ideal as a practice victim; nothing much can go wrong. Calling it a butterfly, as butchers do, is a joke like naming your bloodhound Fifi. Far from being fluttery or ethereal, the lamb is hearty, richly flavored from its marinade, and something like a beef *filet* in texture. The meat firms up as it cooks into a thick juicy slab. We like it rare, firm and dark brown outside and an even bright peony-pink within, and we cut it in thick slices. It's an American technique to butterfly and grill a lamb leg and one which delights and surprises our French guests, who don't even recognize their old friend the *gigot*.

A perfect accompaniment to grilled lamb, and a convenient one since it's good hot or cold, is a dish of topinambours, a vegetable which gardeners tell me grows like a weed and which markets have begun to offer regularly. The word is French, adapted from the Portuguese, which is in turn an alteration of *tupinamba*—short for *batata tupinamba* or tupinamba potato, according to the big Webster's. And according to a French source, the Tupinamba are a small native tribe in Brazil who presumably nourished themselves on the vegetable that bears their name. The vegetable is related to the sunflower family, and since sunflower in French is *girasol,* it is probable that the nickname "Jerusalem artichoke" is a corruption of what was originally "*girasol artichaut.*" But the topinambour vegetable is neither potato, nor is it artichoke. "Sunchoke," as the topinambour is sometimes called, is a modern publicity-stunt name invented to intrigue the buyer and only adds to general confusion. When this delightful vegetable is not available for a barbecue menu, I cook artichokes in a particularly flavorful way (since they too can be served hot or cold and suit lamb very well); see the bonus recipe in the Menu Variations section.

Speaking of names, the Zabaione Batardo Veneziano, which sounds like Iago badmouthing Otello, *basso profondo,* is called "Venetian" because it is based on a lovely concoction we first ate at a hotel in Venice; "Zabaione" because it involves egg yolks beaten with Marsala; and "Batardo" because it is bastardized by being stabilized with gelatin and served cold. Real *zabaione* is just egg yolks, wine, and sugar and is served still warm in a wineglass the moment it's made.

We don't have too leafy a salad, since so many guests enjoy stuffing theirs into a pita pocket: a mixture of bite-sized vegetables with just enough foliage for texture seems to work best. We always did like storebought pita; but then we tried making our own and got addicted. Homemade pita, which you can attend to unhurriedly, permitting two rises and a rest before baking, has a fuller flavor than the store kind and a pleasing tender chewiness—even though it looks like the makings of a snow-

boot, suede-smooth outside and fleecy inside. If you and your guests have had to move indoors, and especially if some of them are teenagers, do take a few unbaked pita disks and some grated cheese from your freezer, add some herbs and some Italian tomato sauce (the storebought kind can be very good), and give them homemade pita pizzas as an effortless extra. Or, if you have a glass-fronted oven or can borrow one of the portable electric ones, you might feature pita baking as a rainy-day double feature. About one minute after the inert white disks go into the oven, at highest heat, they begin to stir mysteriously, swelling and heaving from side to side. At full inflation, the edges lift right off the baking surface and the pita stand on tiptoe as if aspiring to flight. The moment is brief, the striving too strenuous, and they sink back, but only a little: still unbowed, I like to think.

In a similarly poetic mood, my husband one day christened a beautiful and potent emerald-green cocktail of his own invention. Remember the doggerel ballad by one J. Milton Hayes about the dashing young subaltern in Inscrutable India, who stole "The Green Eye of the Yellow God" to gratify the whim of his love, the Colonel's daughter? Alas for impetuous youth! In the rhythm of "Polly-Wolly-Doodle," the verses trot to a melancholy conclusion, for the god took his revenge.

There's a one-eyed yellow idol to the north of Khatmandu,
There's a little marble cross below the town;
There's a broken-hearted woman tends the grave of Mad Carew,
And the Yellow God forever gazes down.
Paul's delicious creation is luckily not so malevolent as its namesake; but be warned. It's every bit as powerful.

Preparations

Recommended Equipment:
If you don't own a charcoal grill, or if you plan to improvise one, I suggest you take a look at the detailed and practical section on outdoor cooking in *Joy of Cooking*, a book that surely needs no introduction. The only equipment specifically needed for doing butterflied lamb over coals is a hinged two-sided rack with a long handle for easy turning. See the pita recipe for a discussion of alternative baking methods.

For the cocktail, the wine, and the dessert, note that you will need 18 goblets.

Marketing and Storage:
Quantities for 6 people
Staples to have on hand

Salt
Peppercorns
Hot pepper sauce
Dry mustard
Rosemary
Cream of tartar
Pure vanilla extract
Soy sauce
Red-wine vinegar
Cooking oil
Olive oil for optional marinade and for salad
  (or use another fine salad oil)
Plain unflavored gelatin (1 package)
Granulated sugar
All-purpose flour (2¾ cups or 390 g),
  unbleached recommended
Plain bleached cake flour (¾ cup or 105 g)
Recommended: Wondra or instant-blending
  flour (⅓ cup or 50 g)
Dry active yeast (1 Tb or 1 package)
Butter (1 stick)
Heavy cream (1 cup or ¼ L, plus more if using
  for dessert decoration)

Eggs (4)
Lemons (2)
Garlic (2 heads)
Parsley and/or chives
Shallots and/or scallions

Specific ingredients for this menu

Leg of lamb (note that a big, 7-pound or 3½-kilo leg will serve 12 to 14 when butterflied)

For optional lamb stock: 1 carrot, 1 onion, 2 or more celery ribs, 1 leek, and an herb bouquet

Topinambours (Jerusalem artichokes or sunchokes), 14 to 18

Romaine (1 medium-size head)

Watercress (1 or 2 bunches)
Red onions (1 medium-size)
Green and/or red sweet peppers (2)
Cherry tomatoes (12 to 18)
Fresh herbs (if possible): tarragon, chervil, basil
Feta cheese (½ pound or 225 g)
For *zabaione* decoration: cocoa or grated chocolate, or home-candied orange peel
Sweetened bottled lime juice (Rose's recommended)
Green crème de menthe (mint liqueur)
Gin
Marsala wine (best quality), ⅛ bottle
Peanuts, to serve with the cocktail

Buddha's Eye

A gin and lime cocktail with green crème de menthe

A strong clean drink to be served in small upstanding stemmed glasses

5 parts gin
2 parts sweetened lime juice (Rose's recommended)
2 parts green crème de menthe (mint liqueur)

Stir all ingredients together in a pitcher with ice cubes and, as soon as well chilled, pour into the glasses.

Butterflied Leg of Lamb

For barbecuing or roasting

To butterfly a leg of lamb means to bone it so that the meat may be spread out in one large piece. You can then barbecue it or roast it, and not only does it cook in half the time of an unbutterflied leg, but carving is wonderfully easy.

Fat removal and bone location

To prepare the lamb, first cut off as much outside fat as you can from all sides of the meat, then shave off the fell (membrane on top side of leg), and it is ready for boning. The whole leg of lamb contains the hipbone and tail assembly at the large end, the main leg bone that slants crosswise from the socket of the hipbone to the knee, and the shank bone from the knee to the ankle at the small end. All the boning takes place on the underside of the leg, not on the top or fell side.

Hipbone

The first and the worst bone to tackle is the hipbone-tail assembly, a complicated and convoluted structure if there ever was one. Lay lamb so its large end faces away from you and plunge fearlessly in with a very sharp, rather short knife; and by always cutting against the bone rather than against the flesh in any boning operation you are doing the right thing. Start at the exposed cut end of the hip that sticks out in the upper middle of the underside at the large end. Cut around under it (the side of the bone facing you, and the small end of the leg), branching out both right and left as well as down, and you will find that it attaches itself at about its middle to the main leg bone: you will gradually uncover the round ball end of the leg bone that fits into the socket of the hip. By cutting around the ball end you will detach its tendons from the hip socket, and then, as you follow on down the hip and cut around under it, you can quite easily detach it from the meat.

Leg bones

With the hip out of the way, do the shank bone next, at the small end of the lamb, starting again on the underside. Cut the meat from the sides of the bone and under it, and proceed up to the knee joint but do not cut around it yet. Now you will make a frank cut in the meat, still from the underside of the lamb, going from the knee joint in a direct line to the ball joint, where you removed the hip. Cut around the main leg bone thus exposed and the knee, being careful not to pierce the flesh on the top side of the meat (although there is no great harm done if you do), and you will free the leg and shank bones in one piece. Cut out the white cartilaginous disk that is the kneecap, as well as all chunks of interior fat.

Final rites

Lay the meat out, boned surface up, on your work surface, and you will note that it forms two large lobes. (If you have a large leg and are serving only 6 people, you may wish to cut off one of the lobes and freeze it for another roast or for shish kebabs.) For even cooking, I always slash the lobes in 2 or 3 places, making long cuts about 1 ½ inches (4 cm) deep; otherwise these thick pieces of meat will take longer to cook than the rest. Then, to keep the roast in shape, I like to push long skewers through the wide sides of the meat, one through the top third, and the other through the bottom third.

🕐   Lamb may be boned and prepared for roasting a day in advance; wrap in plastic and refrigerate.

Optional Marinade:
3 to 4 Tb olive oil
2 Tb soy sauce
The juice of ½ lemon, plus the grated peel if you wish
½ tsp or so rosemary
1 or 2 cloves garlic, puréed (optional)

Rub the unboned side of the lamb with a tablespoon of olive oil and place, oiled side down, in a baking pan. Rub the rest of the oil and the soy, lemon juice and optional peel, rosemary, and optional garlic into the top side. Cover with plastic wrap and marinate until you are ready to cook the lamb—an hour or more, if possible.

Lamb leg (underside) before trimming and after. Note the ball of the leg bone and the socket of the hip.

To barbecue the lamb

When the coals are just right, place the lamb in an oiled, hinged (double-sided) rack and barbecue, turning every 5 minutes or so and brushing with oil, for 45 minutes to an hour, depending on the heat of your coals and the way you like your lamb. If you want it rosy red, it is done when it begins to take on resistance to your finger, in contrast to its soft raw state. A meat thermometer reading would be 125°F/51°C. Remove the lamb to a carving board and let it sit for 8 to 10 minutes, allowing juices to retreat back into the meat before carving. To carve, start at either of the small ends and, to make attractively largish slices, begin somewhat back from the edge, angling your knife as though carving a flank steak (or even a smoked salmon).

To roast in the oven

I prefer to roast the lamb and then finish it off under the broiler. To do so, place the marinated lamb flat, boned side up, in a roasting pan in the upper middle of a preheated 375°F/190°C oven and roast for 20 to 25 minutes, or to a meat thermometer reading of 120°F/49°C. (I do not turn the lamb on its other side.) Then baste with oil and set for 2 to 3 minutes under a preheated broiler to brown lightly. Always let it sit for 8 to 10 minutes outside the oven before carving and carve as suggested in the preceding paragraph.

Save All Bones for Soup or Sauce:

You can make a wonderfully hearty broth out of lamb bones and meaty scraps. Whack the bones into convenient pieces with your cleaver, then brown bones and scraps in a 450°F/230°C oven in a roasting pan with a quartered onion and carrot. Drain off accumulated fat and dump contents of pan into a large saucepan with water to cover. Then deglaze the roasting pan: set it over heat with a cup of water, scrape up coagulated juices, and pour them into the saucepan. Simmer, skim, add a couple of celery ribs, a little salt, an herb bouquet, a leek if you have one, and a clove or two of garlic. Cover partially and simmer 3 hours or so, then strain, degrease, and that's all there is to it. Recipes for sauces are in *Mastering I,* and for soup see *J.C.'s Kitchen.*

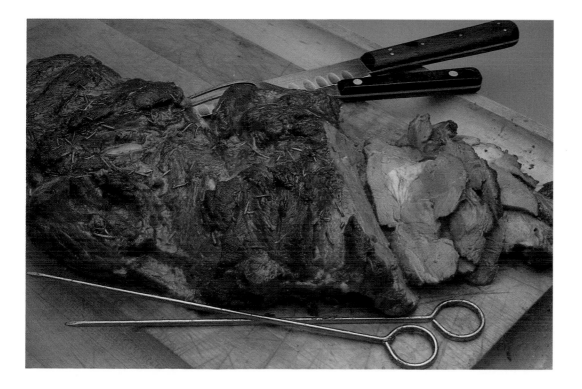

Pita Bread

Armenian, Syrian, or Israeli flat bread
Pita bread, the flat pale bread-dough Near Eastern pancakes that you can separate into two layers, is easy indeed to make when you have constructed yourself a simulated baker's oven. That means you have quarry tiles or a stoneware griddle to set on your oven rack, onto which you slide the dough to bake. Although you can cook pita on top of the stove, the complete puff is not always achieved, and the bottom layer remains thicker than the top layer. And although you can also bake pita on cookie sheets in the oven, it is not as satisfactory as the griddle. Griddles, by the way, are available via many country store catalogues. They are often sold as pizza sets and include a wooden sliding board or baker's peel; the rectangular griddle is the one to order since it is a more useful shape than the round one for breads, rolls, and pita, as well as for pizza. Pita dough makes wonderful pizza, too.

Like homemade English muffins, your own-made pita cost you less than half the price of store-bought ones, in addition to being fun and dramatic to make.

For 12 pita 6 inches in diameter

1 Tb (1 package) yeast dissolved in ½ cup (1 dL) tepid water
About 1 pound (450 g) of flour as follows: 　　2¾ cups (390 g) all-purpose flour, 　　unbleached recommended 　　¾ cup (105 g) plain bleached cake flour
2 tsp salt
1 Tb olive oil or tasteless salad or cooking oil
1 cup (¼ L) tepid water; droplets more as necessary
Equipment
Best, a tile or stoneware baking surface to fit your oven rack; second best, an aluminum baking sheet. A wooden sliding board, shingle, or peel. A long-handled pancake turner. A cake rack or racks for cooling baked pita. A rolling pin.

Making the dough

When yeast is thoroughly dissolved, combine it with the ingredients listed, kneading in enough of the water to make a moderately firm dough. When well blended, let rest for 2 minutes, then knead vigorously until dough is smooth and elastic and does not stick to your hands—5 minutes or more. Place in a clean, fairly straight-sided 4-quart (4-L) bowl, cover, and let rise at 75°F to 80°F (24°C–27°C) until slightly more than doubled in bulk—2 hours or so. Deflate by pulling dough inward from sides of bowl, cover, and let rise again to slightly more than double—about 1½ hours.

🕐 Second rise may be completed in the refrigerator, and when risen, you may punch down dough, cover with a weight to keep it down, and leave for 24 hours—or you may freeze it.

Forming the pita

Turn dough out onto a floured work surface and lengthen it by rolling it back and forth under the palms of your hands, forming a thick sausage shape about 16 inches (40 cm) long. Cut even portions all the same size by halving the dough crosswise, halving the 2 halves, then cutting each of these 4 pieces into thirds. Then, to make the pancake shape more even, first form a cushion out of each piece of dough by bringing the 4 corners together and pinching to seal them, then turn seal side down and roll under the palm of one hand to make a ball; set each aside, as you form it, on a floured corner of your work surface, and cover with a lightly floured sheet of plastic.

These balls of dough are now to be rolled into pancake-size disks which are to rest either on a floured wooden surface or on floured towels for 20 minutes or so while the oven heats. Proceed as follows: one at a time, with a rolling pin on a quite heavily floured surface, roll each ball into a disk ¼ inch (¾ cm) thick

and 6 inches (15 cm) across. Place disk on prepared resting surface, cover with floured plastic, and continue with the rest.

Baking the pita

Set quarry tiles, griddle, or bake sheet in lower middle level of oven, and preheat to 500°F–550°F (260°–270°C)–highest heat! When oven is ready, lightly flour the sliding board, place on it 2 or 3 pita, and slide then onto the hot baking surface. In about 1 minute, large bubbles will appear on surface of the pita and they will then quickly and dramatically puff up like pillows, reach their maximum, and subside slightly. Leave for a moment (baking should take about 2 minutes in all) and remove with a pancake turner before they have time to color or harden. Continue with remaining pita. Let cool completely; they will gradually collapse.

🕐   Leave on rack for an hour or two, then stack together, pressing out air, and store in a plastic bag; refrigerate for 2 to 3 days, or freeze.

Manufacturing Notes:

You may find, as I did, that, although pita are easy to make, it does take a session or two to perfect your techniques. It seems important to watch that the dough is fairly firm, since if it is too soft the disks are sticky to roll and limp to handle. They must be smooth, unwrinkled, and at least ¼ inch (¾ cm) thick, too, or the pita may not puff up into the proper pillow shape.

Pizza:

Roll the pita dough to any size you wish, but the 6-inch (15-cm) pita shape is just right for individual servings. When oven is ready, place 3 or 4 dough disks on lightly floured sliding board, rapidly garnish with the pizza topping of your choice, and slide onto hot baking surface in oven, exactly as though you were baking pita. Topping will prevent dough from puffing, and when bottom is lightly browned, in about 5 minutes, the pizza is done.

Notes on Freezing:

You can roll out the dough into disks, flour the disks, stack each between sheets of plastic wrap, and freeze in a bunch. You can then take them singly from freezer to oven; although they will bake into pita, they do not puff quite as much as when fresh—and whether you bake a pita solidly frozen or thawed seems to make little difference. I find the frozen disks just fine for pizza, however, either frozen or thawed before baking.

Serving Suggestions:

Pita pocket sandwiches. Cut the baked pita in half crosswise, gently pull the two halves apart, and fill with any kind of sandwich mixture, such as a salad, hamburger and trimmings, scrambled eggs, a cooked eggplant and tomato mixture, and so forth. Or make your filling and bake it in the pita pocket.

Toasted pita triangles. Split the pita breads—it is often easiest to cut all around the circumference with scissors to make an even split—and cut into triangles of whatever size you wish. Brush with melted butter and, if you wish, a sprinkling of mixed dried herbs and/or grated Parmesan cheese. Arrange buttered side up on a baking sheet and place for a few minutes in a preheated 350°F/180°C oven to crisp and brown lightly. Serve with soups, salads, cheese, or with drinks.

Topinambours

Also called Jerusalem artichokes or sunchokes

These little knobby roots grow underground like potatoes and do remind one in taste of artichokes, yet they are crisp like water chestnuts when raw, and have a very special and mildly pungent taste of their own when cooked. Hot, buttered, and tossed with parsley or chives, they go nicely indeed with roast lamb—or with roast pork, turkey, or beef, for that matter. Cooked and cold, they make an attractive salad vegetable. Since they discolor rapidly, they should be cooked in a *blanc* (a thin solution of flour and water with salt and lemon), the same way you would boil artichoke bottoms or salsify.

For 6 people as a vegetable course

⅓ cup (¾ dL) flour, preferably the instant-blending kind

6 cups (1½ L) cold water; more if necessary

3 Tb lemon juice

2 tsp salt

14 to 18 topinambours

If serving hot—3 Tb or more butter, salt, pepper, and minced parsley and/or chives
If serving cold—minced shallots, salad or olive oil, fresh lemon juice, salt, pepper, and parsley and/or chives

To make the *blanc* liquid, place the flour in a saucepan and beat in the water gradually, to prevent flour from lumping. Add the lemon juice and salt and bring to the simmer. Set the pan by your work surface, and peel the topinambours one by one (using a small knife and simply removing the little knobs along with the peel). Cut the topinambours into ¼-inch (¾-cm) slices and drop the slices into the *blanc* liquid as you proceed. When all are sliced, bring to the boil and simmer 15 to 20 minutes or until just tender when pierced with a knife. (You will notice a remarkable change in taste, from crisp and raw with no pronounced flavor to cooked and with a definite yet subtle taste that is reminiscent of artichoke, yet utterly and uniquely topinambourish.)

🕐 May be cooked in advance. Leave them in their liquid until you are ready to proceed.

To serve hot

Drain (reserving the cooking liquid for a soup base) and toss gently in a sieve under cold running water. Then melt the butter in a saucepan, add the topinambours, and toss gently to coat with the butter and to heat through. Taste carefully for seasoning, then toss with the herbs and serve.

To serve cold

Drain and wash as described in preceding paragraph, then toss with minced shallots, oil, lemon, salt, pepper, and herbs.

Seasonal Salad

Of romaine, watercress, red onion rings, green and/or red peppers, cherry tomatoes, and feta cheese

This is a salad of the season and needs no formal recipe. One suggestion is to tear the romaine into bite-size pieces, stem the watercress, wrap them together in a damp towel, and place in the refrigerator in a plastic bag several hours before serving. Also some hours before serving, slice the red onions and, to minimize their sting, place the slices in a sieve and run boiling water, then cold water, over them; drain thoroughly and toss in a bowl with a spoonful or two of your salad dressing. Halve, seed, and slice the peppers; refrigerate in a covered bowl. Cut the feta cheese into ½-inch (1½-cm) dice and taste; if salty, soak 10 minutes or so in a bowl of cold water and drain. Toss with freshly ground pepper, thyme, oregano, or a mixture of herbs, and a tablespoon or two of olive oil; let macerate for several hours, tossing once or twice. Shortly before serving, wash, stem, and halve cherry tomatoes; sprinkle lightly with salt. At serving time, toss all ingredients except the cheese together in a big salad bowl with your dressing (see next recipe for suggestions) and with fresh herbs if you have them. Taste, correct seasoning, then fold in ¾ of the cheese cubes, strewing the remainder on top.

Vinaigrette Salad Dressing

I have found the following a useful base for salad dressing made in quantity for a large gathering. Use the best and freshest of everything for success!

For 30 people or more, 3 ½ cups (1 scant liter) dressing

4 Tb minced shallots or scallions

2 Tb dry mustard

5 to 6 shakes hot pepper sauce

Grinds of fresh pepper to taste

1 tsp salt, or to your taste

5 Tb red-wine vinegar; more as needed

2 Tb or more fresh lemon juice

3 cups best-quality olive oil, new fresh peanut oil, or other oil of impeccable quality

Fresh herbs of your choice, such as tarragon, chervil, or basil

Beat all ingredients together in an electric mixer or shake in a large screw-topped jar. Taste carefully, and correct seasoning. After you dress your salad, taste a leaf or two and toss in more salt and pepper if needed.

The following proportions would be about right for 6 to 8 people. Simply reduce accordingly for a smaller number.

2 to 3 tsp minced shallots or scallions

½ tsp dry mustard

Grinds of fresh pepper to taste

¼ tsp salt, or to your taste

1 Tb red-wine vinegar

1 Tb fresh lemon juice

½ cup best-quality olive (or other) oil as above, plus fresh herbs

Beat together with a whisk or shake in a screw-top jar. Correct seasoning to your taste both before and after dressing your salad.

❶ May be made somewhat in advance, but it is never a good idea to let salad dressing sit around for more than a day or two; it loses its freshly made quality.

Zabaione Batardo Veneziano

Mock zabaione

This turns out to be, actually, a Marsala-flavored Bavarian cream. One friendly warning is to watch out when you combine the Marsala custard with the whipped cream at the end: if the custard is warm it will deflate the cream, yet if it is too cold the chilled cream will cause the gelatin in it to set and get lumpy before you complete the folding process.

For about 6 cups, serving 6 to 8

⅓ cup (¾ dL) plus 1 Tb sugar

¾ cup (1 ¾ dL) best-quality sweet Marsala wine in a 6-cup (1 ½-L) saucepan

1 ½ level tsp plain unflavored gelatin

4 egg yolks in a 2-quart or -liter stainless-steel saucepan

1 Tb pure vanilla extract

2 egg whites in a clean dry beating bowl

A pinch of salt and ⅛ tsp cream of tartar

1 cup (¼ L) heavy cream for whipping in a 2-quart or -liter stainless-steel bowl

A large bowl with a tray of ice cubes and water to cover them

Decoration

Whipped cream and/or cocoa or grated chocolate, or home-candied orange peel

Combining Marsala custard ingredients
Stir ⅓ cup (¾ dL) sugar into the Marsala, sprinkle the gelatin on top, and set aside to soften while you assemble the rest of the ingredients listed. Then, with a wire whip, vigorously beat the egg yolks in their saucepan for a minute or two until they are thickened slightly and pale yellow. Now set the

Marsala over moderate heat (but do not bring it to the boil) and stir to dissolve both gelatin and sugar completely, looking carefully to be sure there are no unmelted granules of either in the liquid. Finally, beating the egg yolks with your whip, slowly dribble in the hot Marsala.

Heating the Marsala mixture

The Marsala and egg yolk mixture is now to be thickened over heat like a custard. To do so, set it over a moderately low (but not too low) burner, and beat with your wire whip as it slowly warms. As you beat and heat it the mixture will start to foam, and in a few minutes it will be entirely foamy throughout— keep testing with your impeccably clean finger. When it is too hot for that finger you should almost at the same time see the first wisp of steam rising from the surface, and the custard is done. Remove from heat, and beat vigorously for a minute or two to stop the cooking; beat in the vanilla, and set aside.

Beating egg whites and whipping cream

Beat the egg whites slowly until they begin to foam, then beat in the salt and cream of tartar; gradually increase speed to fast and continue until they form shining peaks, then sprinkle on the tablespoon of sugar and beat vigorously to stiffen them more. Delicately fold them into the warm Marsala custard.

Then whip the cream, setting it in the ice cubes and water, until it has doubled in volume, beater leaves light traces on its surface, and cream holds its shape softly—this is now *crème Chantilly,* or lightly whipped cream.

Combining the elements

Set custard pan in the ice cubes and fold custard delicately (so as not to deflate it) with a rubber spatula, testing continually with your finger just until custard is cool but not cold or chilled. Immediately remove pan from ice and at once fold in the whipped cream to make a beautifully smooth, creamy pale-yellow ambrosia. Turn it either into a serving bowl or into individual goblets, cover, and chill for 2 hours or more.

🕐   May be completed a day or two in advance.

To serve

Decorate with swirls of whipped cream and/or cocoa or grated chocolate—or with a julienne of home-candied orange peel.

⏱ *Timing*

This meal could hardly be easier to plan for. Just before serving time, dress and toss the salad, whip the cream, if you're using it, for the dessert decoration, and reheat the topinambours if you're having them hot. Remember to give the lamb a 10-minute sit after it's cooked; and, if you're cooking indoors, it needs watching during its 3 minutes in the broiler. Oven roasting, with an occasional baste, takes 20 to 25 minutes.

If you're outside, allow an hour, with frequent basting and turning, for the lamb to grill. At least an hour before cooking, set the lamb in its marinade. At that stage start your fire. Any time during the day, wash, dry, and trim the salad makings, prepare the dressing, and cook the topinambours.

You can bone the lamb the day before. The *zabaione* can be made one or two days before, and the pita, two or three. (Or you can freeze the pita dough, made long before; but they don't puff quite so high.)

Menu Variations

The barbecued meat: Other large cuts of meat to marinate and grill would include beef, both steak and roasting cuts, not more than 2 inches (5 cm) thick. You can of course grill chops, and there is always chicken; but, if you are forced indoors, they will have to be done under the broiler and given close attention.

The salad: There are several salad recipes in these menus; with full-flavored meat and wine, have something rather assertive and oniony.

The zabaione: See the Menu Variations in "Informal Dinner" for other custardy desserts you can make ahead of time.

The topinambours: The only other vegetable that remotely resembles topinambours in flavor is the artichoke. See the recipe for preparing artichoke bottoms on page 31. Or forget that flavor altogether and do one of the eggplant recipes in *Mastering II*. Lamb and eggplant go beautifully together.

Sauté of Fresh Artichoke Hearts with Onions and Garlic

Onions and garlic and a whisper of wine vinegar give a special taste to this sauté of artichokes. Serve it hot with roast or barbecued meats, cold as an hors d'oeuvre, or with sausages, or with hard-boiled eggs and sliced tomatoes.

For 6 people as a vegetable accompaniment

6 to 8 fine fresh artichokes
1 lemon
4 Tb or so olive oil
1 head garlic
4 large onions
Salt and pepper
Thyme or mixed dried herbs
2 Tb or so butter
1 to 2 Tb wine vinegar
Minced fresh parsley
Equipment
A heavy deep frying pan or an electric skillet

Preparing the artichokes

Artichoke hearts include the artichoke bottom and the tender part of the inner cone of leaves. When artichokes are very young and fresh, you can use the whole cone without removing the choke; however, it is rare indeed to find such quality outside the artichoke-growing regions. I prepare the usual store bought artichokes as follows, one at a time. Cut the stem off an artichoke, close to the base. Then bend the leaves at right angles to the base until they snap close to their large end; pull down toward the base to snap the leaf off, leaving the tender part of its base attached to the artichoke bottom; continue rapidly until you reach the pale creamy cone of leaves covering the choke. Shave the tough green from around the base of the artichoke, using a small knife at first, then a vegetable peeler. Frequently rub cut portions of artichoke base with half a lemon as you go to prevent discoloration. After trimming you will usually have to cut off the top part of the cone, down to where you judge the tender part begins. Cut the heart in half lengthwise and, if large, in quarters. Scoop out the choke (hairy portion covering bottom) with a small knife, and rub the quarters again with lemon. As soon as one heart is prepared, drop it into your frying pan with the olive oil and set over low heat, tossing to cover with the oil. Continue rapidly with the rest of the artichokes.

The sauté

With the artichokes still over low heat and being tossed now and then (toss by swirling and shaking pan by its handle), separate the cloves of garlic and drop them into a pan of boiling water for a moment to loosen the skins. Peel the cloves, halve or quarter them lengthwise if large, and add to the artichokes. Peel, halve, and slice the onions lengthwise; toss them into the pan with the artichokes and garlic. Season with salt, pepper, and herbs; add 2 tablespoons butter and toss to melt it. Cover the pan and cook slowly until artichokes are just tender when pierced with a knife—20 minutes or so—and toss once or twice. Pour in the vinegar, toss, cover, and cook 5 minutes more. Correct seasoning.

🕐   May be cooked in advance; set aside uncovered and reheat, tossing and adding a little more oil or butter if you wish.

To serve hot

Toss with minced parsley.

To serve cold

Let cool after their initial sauté and, if you wish, chill. Before serving, toss with a little lemon juice, a little olive oil, salt and pepper to taste, and fresh minced parsley.

Leftovers

The barbecued lamb: This is as good cold as it was hot, in slices or sandwiches. If you have only scraps, think of curry, shepherd's pie, hash, or add to a hearty soup based on lamb stock made from the bones (see recipe).

There's little to be said about the other elements in this meal, except to warn you not to keep any eggy mixture, like the *zabaione,* for more than four days unless you freeze it.

Postscript: On eating

In planning meals for company, we all think carefully about our resources of money, kitchen equipment, serving possibilities, and, especially, time. And at the shopping stage we are careful about quality and flexible (if what we wanted isn't there) about varying our menus. Feasible preparation, graceful service, good food: can one ask any more than that?

Yes. One ought, in planning menus, to ponder the act of eating as much as the food itself. One of the nice things about this barbecue, for instance, is the agreeable option for guests of stuffing a pita pocket with salad, mingling moist and dry, crunchy and chewy, sharp and bland for that first alligator-size bite. Instruments and gestures matter: the light supple grasp of chopsticks, for instance, affords a sensation different from the stab and leverage of a fork: which one suits your menu? What happens to a mouthful? A cannelated tube doesn't merely make a purée prettier; the tongue delights in smoothing the little corduroy ridges to velvet.

Eating wasn't done with the fingers when I was young, except with bread, corn on the cob, and, in some parts of the country, asparagus. I have come to wonder if all the *do*'s and *don't*'s about eating, rather than the anxiously cramming mothers the shrinks love to belabor, weren't the reason why so many children had "feeding problems" then. How *could* anybody not love to eat, unless it had always been made a penance?

I agree, of course, that table manners are important. Dribblers, twiddlers, spillers, garglers, smokers at meals, and panters are unwelcome company. And such legerdemain as filleting a sautéed trout or carving a squab (a bird I really prefer, however, to eat in gluttonous solitude) is as pleasant to watch as to perform. During one stay in Rome, Paul and I went daily to the same little trattoria expressly to watch one of their regular clients' beautifully deft way with the peeling of whole oranges and pears, and the neat dismemberment of small spit-roasted birds; his awareness of our admiration seemed to stimulate him to heights of virtuosity.

But it would have been a pointless performance if the old gentleman hadn't eaten with such relish. Food like love is a deeply emotional matter. Intrusive or assertive displays aside, do you really mind, do you find indecent, the sight of intense bliss, of a child's pointed pink tongue molding the ice cream in a cone, of a friend's half-closed eyes and expanded nostrils as he inhales the scent of your good brandy? Isn't there joy in the sound of a fork's first break into a puff pastry, and a doomsday note in the expiring gurgle of a chocolate soda's last drop on its way up the straw?

I like to watch my guests eat and to imagine their pleasure in the lobster's clawlets as they suck, or in something so simple as the smoothness, form, and heft of a hard-boiled egg. I think of Muriel Spark's loving glimpse in *Memento Mori* of a grandmother feeding a baby, her mouth moving in unconscious sympathy as he eats. Nominally about death, that novel is about the preciousness of life, and so, however modestly, is every honest cookbook.

Bon appétit, then... and *vive la compagnie!*

A meal you'd cook for (and maybe with) other cooks. Plus talk of mussels

UFOs in Wine

Eating this meal demands fingers, and cooking it demands loving, last-minute attention. The right people to ask to this dinner party are knowing, sensuous eaters whom you welcome backstage because they understand and enjoy what's going on there. Dine in the kitchen, if you have room, so your friends can breathe in that first waft of perfumed steam when you uncover the mussel pot. Let them await in suspense that soul-satisfying plop when the big potato pancake is flipped in sizzling butter. And don't feel rushed arranging the main course stylishly; it only takes a moment, and is served all on one platter except perhaps for the cherry tomatoes. (Big tomatoes wouldn't, I feel, be in the right scale for these small birds on their neat round nest.)

A *paillasson,* or straw mat, is what the birds' nest looked like to Fernand Point when he used to serve the straw potato *galette* at his legendary restaurant, La Pyramide, in southern France. According to Point's former apprentice, chef Joe E. Hyde, in his engaging cookbook *Love, Time, and Butter* (New York: Richard W. Baron, 1971), Point's version was cooked first on the stove, and then the frying pan was moved to the oven. But that was before the blessed advent of nonstick cooking utensils.

As to the Flying Objects, they truly are Unidentified, as this recipe works well for many kinds of small birds. But since squab pigeons, partridge, quail, etc., are rather hard to come by, and the season for game birds is short anyway, I chose Rock Cornish hens. Just for fun, I looked up their origin in the *Encyclopaedia Britannica,* and discovered that in the late eighteenth century cocks were imported here from Cornwall and mated with our Plymouth

Rock hens. So it's an old breed, though we didn't hear much about it until the middle of this century. I think the first person to have raised Rock Cornish commercially was the humorist-cum-pianist Victor Borge, at his farm in Connecticut. For some years you could buy them only frozen, but growing demand has made fresh Rock Cornish hens more and more available. At about a pound, a hen serves one jumbo or two standard-sized guests. Mussels, though not a bit fattening, are so filling that I figure, for the next course, half a hen is better than one.

These elegant birds have a slightly more pronounced flavor than does chicken, but it's still mild; so I step it up with a marinade (which you wouldn't need with a squab or a wild bird) and intensify it by cooking them under a light blanket of shredded Swiss cheese.

UFOs — in this case fresh Cornish hens — being arranged on their straw potato galette

That might sound odd, but you don't taste the cheese as such — you just taste the bird more, and of course it browns beautifully. I use a good nutty Gruyère, sometimes mixed with mozzarella, almost as freely as butter — not so much for its own very unassertive flavor as for the way it enhances others. The marinade is quickly turned into a savory little sauce, and the mushrooms and garlic are strewn over all. Don't worry about the garlic: blanching and roasting tame it down.

Fresh fruit is a perfect follow-up to such richly flavored first and second courses, and it should be something not too sweet, with the tang of citrus and a soft plumpness for contrast. Above all, after such an artful, even whimsical dish as the birds on their nest, the dessert should be pretty but matter-of-fact.

Our friend Rosie said delightedly, "This is such a *foody* meal!" and it is, if you see what we mean. The precise word for it, though, occurs only in French — *raffiné,* meaning 1 part refined, 2 parts canny, 3 parts subtle, plus 1 dash amusing: a nice cocktail of an adjective.

Preparations and Marketing

Recommended Equipment:

To steam the mussels, use an 8-quart (8-L) soup kettle with a lid; enamel or stainless steel is preferable to aluminum, which turns wine gray. You'll need something to dip the mussels out with.

For the potato *galette,* a nonstick frying pan 11 or 12 inches (28 to 30 cm) in top diameter, with some kind of cover, and a long-handled pancake turner. Be sure the well of your serving platter matches or exceeds the frying pan in size.

The tomatoes should have a sauté pan just big enough to hold them in one layer.

Before clarifying butter, don't forget to check your cheesecloth supply.

Staples to Have on Hand:

Salt
Peppercorns
Sugar
Optional: fragrant dried tarragon
Imported bay leaves
Flour
Optional: olive oil

Corn syrup
Chicken stock or broth ▼
Shallots or scallions
Butter
Clarified butter ▼
Carrots (1)
Onions (4 or 5)
Celery (1 small stalk with leaves)
Parsley
Port or Madeira wine
Dry white French vermouth or dry white wine
Orange liqueur

Specific Ingredients for This Menu:

Mussels (5 to 6 pounds; about 4 quarts or
   4 L) ▼
Rock Cornish hens (3), fresh preferred
Swiss (Gruyère) cheese (1 cup or ¼ L, grated;
   about ½ pound or 225 g)
Garlic (2 or more heads)
Mushrooms (1 pound or 450 g)
Potatoes (6 medium), "baking" type preferred
Ripe cherry tomatoes (36 to 48) ▼
Fresh green herbs, such as parsley, chives,
   tarragon, or chervil
Seedless oranges (5 or 6 large "navel" type)
Blueberries (1 pint or ½ L), fresh or frozen

▶ **Remarks:**
Staples to have on hand
Chicken stock or broth: the recipe for making it is in this chapter; you can, however, use canned broth. *Clarified butter:* the recipe for it is on page 110. We treat it as a staple because it's so good to have on hand all the time, and it keeps for months refrigerated.
   Specific ingredients for this menu
Mussels: moules marinière begins with fresh, live mussels in their shells. Before you buy them, please read the note preceding the recipe; a few hints on gathering your own mussels are given in the Postscript to this chapter. *Cherry tomatoes:* since you can rarely buy them perfectly ripe, allow a few days' lead time.

De-bearding a mussel

Mussels:

Quantity note: for the average-sized mussels commercially sold, you can figure that 1 quart equals 1½ pounds (675 g) equals 25 mussels in the shell equals 1 cup (¼ L) mussel meat. This rule of thumb comes from Sarah Hurlburt.

Preparing mussels for cooking

Mussels are perishable, and you should plan to cook them as soon as possible after buying or gathering them. The latter will need more cleaning than cultivated mussels. First, wash the mussels. Then, with a short, stout knife, scrape off any seaweed, barnacles, etc. Pull off their wispy beards as illustrated. Discard any mussels that do not quickly close when tapped, any mussels with cracked or broken shells, any that feel unduly light (they may be empty), or any that feel unusually heavy (they may be full of sand).

Soak the mussels (whether cultivated or gathered) in a bowl of cold water, swishing and knocking them about with your hands for a few seconds, and let them sit for 5 minutes. Lift them out, and if there is any sand at the bottom of the bowl, rinse out and repeat the process, doing so several times if need be. Since there is nothing worse than sandy mussels, I also take a final step: I put 4 or 5 tablespoons of flour in the bottom of a bowl, blend it with cold water, then fill the bowl with 4 quarts or so (4 L) cold water, add the mussels, swish about again, and let them sit for 15 to 20 minutes—the theory being that they eat the flour and while doing so disgorge the rest of their sand. (I am sorry to report that, despite all you can do, you will once in a while run into a batch of mussels that are gritty—Sarah Hurlburt, author of *The Mussel Cookbook* (Cambridge: Harvard University Press, 1977), tells me this is caused, strangely enough, by eider duck droppings in the seawater near mussel beds. Some kind of a chemical reaction then irritates the mussels, and they produce calcium granules in their flesh, like tiny oysters. Too bad, if this happens; but you can steam them open, as in the following recipe, and use their juices, and perhaps even purée and strain the meat.)

Swish and jostle the mussels in clear, then floury, water so they will disgorge their sand.

Moules Marinière

Mussels steamed in wine, minced onions, and parsley

For 6 people as a first course

5 to 6 pounds (about 4 quarts or 4 L) mussels, prepared as in the preceding directions

3 to 4 Tb butter

1 cup (¼ L) minced onion

3 to 4 Tb minced shallots (optional)

1 or 2 cloves garlic, minced (optional)

A large handful of fresh chopped parsley

About 2 cups (½ L) dry white wine or dry white French vermouth

Equipment:

An 8-quart (8-L) stainless-steel or enamel (not aluminum) soup kettle with lid, and a perforated scoop

Prepare the mussels as described. A few minutes before serving time, melt the butter in the kettle, stir in the onion and optional shallots and garlic, and cook slowly for 4 or 5 minutes, until wilted. Then add the parsley and the mussels; cover kettle and shake to mix mussels with the rest of the ingredients. Pour in the wine or vermouth, and shake again. Turn heat to high, cover kettle tightly, and let steam for 3 to 4 minutes (do not shake again or you may toss sand into the mussels), until the mussels are open. As soon as they open, they are done.

Dip the mussels, shells and all, into a big serving bowl or into individual soup bowls. Let liquid settle for a minute in kettle, then pour liquid, and spoon onion and parsley, over mussels, being careful not to add any sand that may be in the bottom of the kettle.

To eat the mussels

To eat the mussels, use your fingers, plucking the mussels out of their shells. Or, for slightly more elegance, after eating one with your fingers, use the shells from that mussel as pincers to pick the meat out of the rest. Either pile the shells neatly interlaced at the edge of your bowl or have a shell dish at your side, then spoon up their delicious juices, like a soup.

🕐   Mussels should be served as soon as they are cooked; they will toughen and dry out if you attempt to keep them warm. However, this recipe is a starting point for many other delicious preparations, including the mussel soup and the mussels in mayonnaise on the half shell described later in the chapter.

Rock Cornish Hens Broil-roasted in Wine

This is a fine recipe for any small young birds—like pigeon, quail, partridge—and is particularly good with fresh Rock Cornish game hens.

For 6 people

3 Rock Cornish hens (1 pound or 450 g each)

Ingredients for Brown Poultry Stock and Sauce:

1 medium carrot and onion, chopped

1½ cups (3½ dL) chicken stock or broth

½ cup (1 dL) dry white wine or dry white French vermouth

1 imported bay leaf

1 small stalk celery with leaves

Ingredients for Optional Marinade:

Salt and pepper

1½ tsp fragrant dried tarragon

2 Tb finely minced shallots or scallions

About ½ cup (1 dL) dry white wine or dry white French vermouth

3 to 4 Tb light olive oil (optional)

Other Ingredients:

Salt and pepper

Melted butter, or clarified butter

1 or more heads garlic

About 1 cup (¼ L) coarsely grated Swiss cheese

½ cup (1 dL) or so Port or Madeira wine, or dry white French vermouth

1 pound (450 g) fresh mushrooms, trimmed, washed, and quartered

2 Tb or more butter for sauce enrichment (optional)

Preparing the hens

(The birds are to be split down the back and spread out, browned under the broiler on both sides, then sprinkled with cheese, surrounded with wine and garlic cloves, and baked until done. The mushrooms are added during the last minutes of cooking.) With

shears or a sharp knife, cut down each side of the backbone from neck to tail, and remove backbone. (Chop the backbone into 2 or 3 pieces and reserve for stock, later.) Turn the birds flesh side up and pound breast flat with your fist. To tuck drumsticks into slits in lower breast skin as shown, first bend knees and push up to shoulders, then tuck ends in. Fold wings akimbo behind backbone each side.

Brown Poultry Stock for Sauce:

For about 1½ cups (3½ dL)
Brown the reserved backbones, necks, and giblets (if any) and the chopped carrot and onion in a frying pan with a little oil or clarified butter (page 110). Scrape into a saucepan, discard browning oil, and rinse frying pan with the stock or broth to dislodge all flavorsome browning particles; pour liquid into saucepan. Add the wine or vermouth, ingredients from the optional marinade, bay leaf, and celery. Bring to the simmer, skim off surface scum for a few minutes, then cover pan loosely and simmer slowly for 1 to 1½ hours. Strain, skim off surface fat, and stock is ready to use.

🕐   May be prepared ahead; refrigerate in a covered jar when cold, or freeze.

Plain Poultry Stock—Chicken Stock:

To make a plain stock simply omit the browning of the ingredients. You may even omit the vegetables altogether, and simmer the carcass bones and scraps, raw or cooked, in lightly salted water.

Put legs through slits in lower edge of breast skin to make a neat shape.

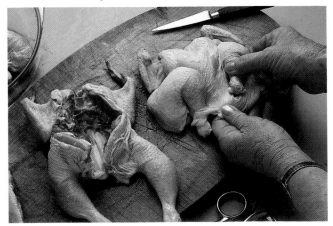

Optional Marinade:

A simple wine marinade will give the usually mild Cornish hens more flavor. Salt and pepper them on both sides and sprinkle with tarragon. Arrange in a bowl, sprinkling each with shallots or scallions, wine, and optional olive oil (oil distributes the flavors of the marinade). Cover and, if kitchen is warm, refrigerate. Marinate for 3 to 4 hours (or longer), turning and basting the birds with the marinade several times. When you are ready to proceed, scrape off marinade and reserve in bowl; dry the birds with paper towels.

Browning under the broiler

Having dried the birds (salt and pepper them lightly if you did not marinate them), brush with melted butter and arrange in one layer skin side down in a broiling or roasting pan. Preheat broiler and set pan so surface of meat is about 3 inches (8 cm) from heat source; brown, basting several times with melted butter, for about 5 minutes on the flesh side; turn, and brown nicely on skin side.

🕐   Recipe may be completed several hours in advance to this point. Although you can refrigerate them, it is best to leave the hens at room temperature if wait is not too long and kitchen not too warm.

After initial browning, sprinkle hens with grated cheese.

Other activities before roasting

Separate garlic cloves and drop into a saucepan of boiling water; simmer 3 or 4 minutes to soften slightly, then slip off the skins and reserve garlic in a small bowl. Grate the cheese, set out the wine, and prepare the mushrooms.

Roasting

About ½ hour at 400°F/205°C

Preheat oven in time for roasting, and plan to roast 30 to 40 minutes before serving. Salt and pepper the skin side of the birds lightly, divide the cheese over them, and strew the garlic around them. Pour in enough wine to film pan by about ¼ inch (¾ cm). Place pan in upper middle level of oven. Baste every 6 minutes or so with the liquids in the pan as the birds slowly brown on top. After about 20 minutes, strew the mushrooms around the birds, basting with liquids in pan. Continue until birds are tender when thighs are pierced with a sharp-pointed fork; juices should run clear yellow with no trace of rosy color.

Finishing the sauce

(I didn't have time for this on our television show, but here is how I would have liked to have done it.) Remove the birds to their platter, arrange around them the mushrooms and half the garlic, scooped out with a slotted spoon. Keep warm for a few minutes in turned-off oven, door ajar, while you complete the sauce. Pour the brown poultry stock into the roasting pan and set over high heat to dislodge any roasting juices, scraping them up with a wooden spoon. Strain them into a small saucepan, leaving garlic in sieve. Skim surface fat off liquid, and rub garlic through sieve with wooden spoon, scraping it off bottom of sieve into the liquid—garlic purée will thicken the liquid as you rapidly boil it down for a moment to concentrate its flavor. When lightly thickened, taste sauce carefully for seasoning. Off heat, if you wish, beat in the enrichment butter by spoonfuls.

Serving

For this menu, the birds are arranged on a giant potato *galette* (following recipe), with the mushrooms and garlic. Either spoon the sauce over the hens, or pass in a warm bowl.

Giant Straw Potato Galette

An enormous pancake of matchstick-sized potato pieces

Potatoes cut into matchstick-sized pieces and pressed into a layer in a large frying pan with hot butter, cooked to a fine walnut brown on each side—what a beautiful bed for our little birds, or for many another morsel, like chops, tournedos, or even fried eggs.

Manufacturing Note:

Potatoes are odd creatures indeed, and one of their peculiarities is that some turn brownish or reddish almost while you are cutting them. Although a sojourn in cold water usually brings them back to white again, the water soaks out the starch—which

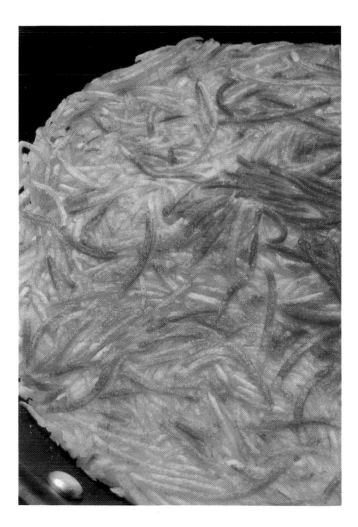

you need for this recipe because you want the potatoes to stick together and form a mat as they cook; no starch and they tend to separate. Thus potato cutting must be a last-minute affair. The cooking of the *galette* is, too; if it sits around, its tender inner core begins to discolor, and the whole *galette* slowly loses its buttery freshly cooked potato taste. Finally, clarified butter is really a must here, since ordinary butter, with its milky residue, can make the potatoes stick to the pan, which spells certain disaster. An excellent way to clarify butter is described on page 110.

For a 9- to 10-inch (23- to 25-cm) galette serving 6 people

About 6 medium potatoes, preferably "baking"

6 Tb or more clarified butter (page 110)

Salt and pepper

Equipment:

A nonstick frying pan 11 to 12 inches (28 to 30 cm) top diameter; a cover of some sort for the pan; a long-handled pancake turner; a round serving platter to hold the galette

Just before you are to cook the *galette,* peel the potatoes, drop into a bowl of cold water, and then cut them into matchstick-sized pieces: either use a big knife, slicing them first, and cutting the slices into sticks; or use the coarse side of a hand grater; or use the grating attachment of a food processor. Do not wash the potatoes once cut; simply dry them in a kitchen towel.

As soon as the potatoes are cut and dried, film the frying pan with a ¹/₁₆-inch (¼-cm) layer of clarified butter, and heat to very hot but not browning. Turn in the potatoes, making a layer about ⅜ inch (1 cm) thick. Sprinkle with salt and pepper, and 2 or 3 spoonfuls more butter, then press them down firmly all over with the spatula so they will mat together as they cook. Frequently press them down while they slowly brown on the bottom, and shake pan gently by its handle to be sure potatoes are not sticking to the pan.

When browned, in 2 to 3 minutes, cover the pan and lower heat to moderate. Cook for 6 to 8 minutes, or until the potatoes are tender on top, but watch they do not burn on the bottom. Press them down again, and the *galette* is ready to brown on its other side.

To turn it: either slide it out onto an oiled baking sheet, turn the frying pan upside down over it, and reverse the two so the *galette* drops into the pan, browned side up; or flip the *galette* in its pan, which, of course, is much more fun and faster—just have the courage to do it! Raise heat slightly, and brown lightly on the other side (which will never show, but browning crisps it). Slide the *galette* onto its platter, and plan to serve it as soon as possible.

🕐   May be kept warm, uncovered, but the sooner you serve it, the better.

Cherry Tomatoes Tossed in Butter and Herbs

Cherry tomatoes, for this delicious recipe, are peeled and then tossed gently in butter, salt, pepper, and herbs just to warm through but not to burst, before serving. A labor indeed it is, but well worth it for beloved family and special friends.

For 6 people—6 to 8 tomatoes apiece

36 to 48 ripe red firm cherry tomatoes

2 Tb or more butter

3 to 4 Tb fresh green herbs, such as parsley, chives, tarragon, and chervil—alone or mixed

Salt and pepper

Equipment:

A nonstick stainless-steel or enamel frying pan just large enough to hold tomatoes in one layer

A handful at a time, drop tomatoes into a saucepan of boiling water and boil 3 or 4 seconds, just enough to loosen the skins. With a small sharp-pointed knife, cut around each stem to remove it, and slip off the skin.

🕐 May be done several hours in advance; place tomatoes in one layer in a glass or enamel plate, cover, and refrigerate.

Just before serving, heat the butter to bubbling in the frying pan, turn in the tomatoes, and roll over heat (shaking and twirling pan by its handle) with the herbs and seasonings just until warmed through. Turn into a hot vegetable dish (or spoon around your meat or vegetable platter); serve at once.

Orange Blueberry Bowl

For 6 people

5 or 6 large fine bright firm ripe seedless "navel" oranges

Sugar syrup: 1 cup (¼ L) sugar, 5 Tb water, and 1 Tb corn syrup

1 pint (½ L) blueberries, fresh or frozen

Sugar, as needed

2 Tb or more orange liqueur

Candied Orange Peel—for Decoration: With a vegetable peeler, remove in strips the orange part of the peel of 3 (or all) of the oranges, and scrape off any white residue from underside of peel. Cut the peel into very fine juliennne strips—as fine as possible. Drop into

1 quart (1 L) simmering water and simmer 10 to 15 minutes, or until tender. Drain, and rinse in cold water; pat dry in paper towels.

Meanwhile, bring the 1 cup (¼ L) sugar, water, and corn syrup to the boil in another saucepan (doubling syrup ingredients if you have used all the orange peel), twirling pan by its handle until sugar has dissolved completely and liquid is perfectly clear. Then cover pan and boil over high heat for a few minutes until syrup has reached the soft-ball stage, 238°F/115°C (bubbles are big and thick, and droplets of syrup form soft balls in cold water). Drop the peel into the syrup and boil slowly for several minutes, until syrup has thickened again. Set aside until ready to use.

🕐   May be done weeks in advance, and stored in a covered jar in the refrigerator.

Preparing the oranges and blueberries
Not more than a few hours before serving, neatly trim off the white part of the peel from the oranges to expose the orange flesh. Cut the oranges into neat crosswise slices, and, if you are not serving for more than an hour, place slices in a bowl, cover, and re-frigerate. Defrost the blueberries if necessary; if they need sugar, toss in a bowl with several tablespoons of sugar and let macerate, covered, in the refrigerator.

Assembling the dessert
Not more than an hour before serving, drain the candied peel, reserving the syrup. Choose an attractive glass serving bowl or individual coupes, and arrange a layer or 2 of orange slices in the bottom, spoon over them a little of the orange peel syrup, and add a few drops of orange liqueur. Drain the blueberries and sprinkle a layer on top of the oranges. Continue to build up the dessert in layers, ending with a handful or 2 of candied orange peel strewn on top. Cover and refrigerate until serving time.

🕐   If the dessert is assembled too soon, the blueberries exude purple coloring down into the oranges—in case that bothers you! And sliced oranges lose their fresh taste as they sit about.

Scrape away all the white from the peel to make the zest.

Before slicing, cut away all peel to expose the juicy flesh of the oranges.

⏱ *Timing*

This is not at all an ahead-of-time meal, and that is certainly one of its charms. Your guests will be getting the finest kind of food freshly cooked and served at once. That means there will be last-minute work for the cook before every course except the dessert. If you have a big family-style kitchen/dining room, you can finish practically all the main cooking right there with your guests, doing only the preliminaries before they come—such as the marination of the birds, the cleaning of the mussels, the peeling of garlic, and the candying of the orange peel. But if you haven't that kind of a kitchen, you'll need to do some planning, as follows.

Last-minute items are the mussels, but they take only 5 minutes or so to steam, plus 4 to 5 minutes to wilt the onions, and while you are cooking them you can finish the sauce for the birds and give the potato *galette* its final flip.

The roasted birds can wait, so they can be finished just before the guests arrive; keep them warm in a turned-off oven, its door ajar, reheating them briefly if need be just before serving. The potatoes could be started at this time, too. And the tomatoes could be given a preliminary toss, but set aside off heat—to be finished just before you serve them.

You'd start roasting the birds half an hour before the guests are to arrive, and preheat the oven 15 minutes before that. Since you need to be around to baste the birds frequently, you could be arranging the dessert at that time, and getting out anything else that you will need.

Scrub the mussels and start their soaking in mid-afternoon. Peel and slice the oranges at this time, too.

This brings us up close to dinnertime again. Backtracking to midday or even morning, you can give the birds their preliminary browning (or marinate them at this point and brown them later), prepare the garlic and mushrooms, peel the cherry tomatoes, and defrost the blueberries, if you're using frozen ones.

The day before, you can buy fresh Rock Cornish hens, prepare them for their cooking, and marinate them. Also, you could simmer their backbones, necks, and giblets for stock; otherwise, make it any time and freeze. If you can buy only frozen birds, be sure to allow 2 days for defrosting in the refrigerator—always the best way. The orange syrup can be prepared now, or even weeks before, from the skins of oranges you may be using for other things.

Even though the cooking of each dish is done at the last, this is not a tricky meal. There are no surprises, and it's unusually delicious as well as being special.

Menu Variations

Moules marinière: there's a variant recipe, thickened with bread crumbs, in *Mastering I,* which has several other classic mussel recipes. That book was intended to explain the dishes and methods my co-authors and I thought most important in traditional French cooking, where mussels count for a lot. But I didn't do anything more about mussels until the frabjous day when they became generally available in this country. Now, joyously making up for the lean years, I have tucked in two more mussel recipes at the end of this section. However, if your fish dealer is still in a rut and you can't get these wonderful shellfish but like the *marinière* idea, you might try clams, as the Italians do: use steamers. I do think a hot, fairly substantial shellfish dish makes an exciting opener for the

Cherry tomatoes tossed in butter and herbs

little birds, but I wouldn't come on too strong. Bouillabaisse, for instance, would be just too much garlic at one meal, but a small serving of Mediterranean fish soup, scallop soup, broiled oysters or a small oyster stew, or a little crab or lobster in mayonnaise would be fine.

Game hens: for a classic dish, *coquelets sur canapés,* roast the birds and serve them with a deglazing sauce on sautéed bread *canapés* (sofas, literally), spread with a pâté made of their livers. Substitute other birds, as the recipe explains, or you can use Rock Cornish hens in many chicken recipes. They're nice served cold, with liver stuffing and Cumberland sauce.

Potato galette: with small birds, crisp potatoes are classic. Homemade potato chips are exquisite, as are waffled potatoes (you need a special cutter), or sautéed potatoes or *pommes soufflées,* for which you can do most of the work beforehand; the final frying in very hot fat goes fast.

Cherry tomatoes: I love the trim look of each guest's plate at this party; but any other lively-tasting, lively-looking vegetable would be nice with the birds.

Fruit desserts: surely you'd want something cold and fresh after *moules marinière* and roast birds with garlic; it's just a matter of the season. Fresh pineapple might be lovely; or a basket of perfect ripe fruit, such as pears, peaches, apricots—it's about the most voluptuous dessert you can offer, yet has a country air like the birds on their nest. Or a bowl of cherries layered with ice to make their skins snap when you bite.

Leftovers

You won't have much in the way of leftovers in this meal. Mussels can go in a salad or soup, as described in the next section.

Bird bones and tomatoes, mushrooms and garlic are also candidates for soup. The potatoes have no future but—oranges and blueberries for breakfast? And now for more mussels!

Soupe aux Moules

Mussel soup

Moules marinière can turn themselves into a perfectly delicious soup, delicate, fragrant with a variety of thinly cut vegetables, and tasting subtly of wine and cream with a tiny spark of curry for the *je ne sais quoi* chic a good soup should have.

For about 2 quarts (2 L)

2 large carrots
2 medium onions
1 or 2 leeks (optional)
2 or 3 celery stalks
6 Tb butter, more if desired
2 cucumbers
Salt and pepper
The recipe for mussels steamed in wine, mussels removed from shells, and cooking liquid with onion and parsley warmed (without sand!)
2 tsp curry powder
4 Tb flour
2 cups (½ L) or more milk, or as needed
2 egg yolks
5 Tb or more heavy cream
Minced fresh parsley

The vegetables

Cut the carrots into julienne matchsticks, and the onions into slices about the same size. Discard roots and tough green parts of leeks, slit leeks lengthwise halfway from root end, turn and slit again; wash, spreading leaves under cold running water, and cut into julienne; cut the celery likewise. Simmer these vegetables slowly in a heavy-bottomed saucepan with 2 tablespoons butter, until wilted but not browned. Meanwhile, peel the cucumbers, cut in half lengthwise, scoop out seeds with a teaspoon, and cut cucumbers into julienne. When other vegetables are almost done, stir in the cucumbers, and salt lightly to taste. Continue cooking for 3 to 4 minutes, then stir in a cupful of mussel-cooking juice and simmer 5 minutes to blend flavors.

The soup base

In a 3- to 4-quart (3- to 4-L) heavy-bottomed stainless-steel saucepan, melt the rest of the butter, blend in the curry and flour, and stir over moderately low heat until butter and flour foam and froth together for 2 minutes without coloring. Remove from heat, and when the *roux* has stopped bubbling, pour in a ladleful of warm mussel liquid; blend vigorously with a wire whip. When smooth, beat in the rest of the liquid, adding enough milk to make about 2 quarts (2 L). Bring to the simmer, stirring slowly with wire whip, and simmer 2 minutes. Fold in the cooked vegetables, simmer several minutes; taste and carefully correct seasoning.

Blend the egg yolks in a medium-sized bowl with 5 tablespoons cream. By dribbles beat in a ladleful of hot soup, then pour the mixture back into the soup. Bring just to the simmer, stirring, so that the yolks may cook and thicken in the soup. Fold the mussels into the soup.

🕐 May be completed to this point. Film top with a spoonful or 2 of milk or cream to prevent a skin from forming. When cool, cover and refrigerate.

To serve

Bring just to the simmer. Correct seasoning again, thin out with milk or cream if necessary, and, if you wish, stir in a little more cream and/or butter. Ladle into soup bowls or a big tureen, and decorate bowls or tureen with a sprinkling of parsley.

Variations:

This soup is very good in itself, even without mussels, using chicken stock or clam juice. Or you could add oysters and fish stock, or diced raw sole or trout fillets that cook for a few minutes in the soup. Or poach scallops in wine and shallots, dice them, and add with their cooking juices to the soup.

Creamy wine-flavored mussel soup with its julienne of vegetables

Moules Farcies

Mussels on the half shell with herbed mayonnaise

For 54 mussels, serving 6 people as a first course

About 3½ pounds (2½ quarts or 2½ L) mussels steamed in wine (about ½ the recipe given earlier in the chapter)
1½ cups (3½ dL) homemade mayonnaise (page 111)
½ cup (1 dL) sour cream
2 Tb finely minced shallots or scallions
1 tsp curry powder (optional)
2 Tb very finely minced parsley
1 Tb very finely minced fresh dill (or a big pinch dried dill weed)
Salt and pepper
Drops of hot pepper sauce

Remove the cooked mussels from their shells but save one of the shells from each mussel. (Save mussel liquid for soup or sauce, or freeze it.) Blend the mayonnaise in a mixing bowl with the sour cream and other ingredients, and taste very carefully for seasoning, adding what else you think would enhance the mayonnaise without masking the delicate taste of the mussels. Place mussels in another bowl, and fold in as much mayonnaise as needed to enrobe them.

🕐 May be prepared in advance several hours before serving; cover and refrigerate.

Shortly before serving time (so mayonnaise topping will not crust over), spoon a sauced mussel into each shell and arrange on special shellfish plates, or on plates lined with shredded lettuce.

🕐 *Ahead-of-Time Note:* Because of the mayonnaise crusting problem, you often find, on buffet setups, that the mussels are prepared with the mayonnaise and then coated with a film of aspic, which seals them. Another solution is to spread finely chopped hard-boiled eggs and parsley over each, on a rack set over a tray, then to arrange the mussels on their dish or dishes.

Variations:

Instead of serving the mussels in their shells, heap them into serving shells and decorate with watercress, or with whatever else you wish. Or mound them into tomato shells, or serve them in a dish as part of a cold platter. Or spoon them around a cold poached fish, or make them part of the cold fish platter. Or fold them into cold cooked rice or pasta. And so forth . . .

Postscript: More on mussels

This chapter's so long I'll try telegraphese. Mussel is: *Mytilus edulis,* edible bivalve, familiar foodstuff worldwide. Consumed in U.S. by coastal Indians, witness prehistoric shell middens; appreciated by Pilgrims, early settlers. Seemingly forgotten, eighteenth to mid-twentieth centuries. Rediscovered, now sold quick-frozen, canned, pickled.

Why? Many virtues. Mussel is: (1) *Delicious!* and adaptable; (2) Not an acquired taste—liked even by shellfish neophytes; (3) Satisfying. Dieters note: 25 mussels (1 quart or 1½ pounds in shell) = 235 calories meat, feels like big meal; (4) Profuse. Cultivated by Spanish method (ropes hung from rafts), 1 acre sea gives 1,000 times as much meat as 1 acre pasture gives beef. Diet of future Americans need not be algae, bean sprouts. Absurd neglect of great resource.

Mussel life-style: efficient. Low on food chain, all bivalves filter seawater; mussels especially "good doers," since filter more. Plankton, other nutrients, unwastefully converted into flesh. Unfussy mussel tolerates high or low salinity; has freshwater, riverbed cousin, also edible but used chiefly for mother-of-pearl shell lining; all mussels also make pearls, not valuable.

Natural beds often several acres, containing millions; occur on Atlantic coast south to Cape Hatteras, on Pacific, south to Mexico. U.S. should cultivate on large scale, like Spain, France, Holland. To harvest own mussels: plumpest to be found below low-tide mark, where submerged, hence eating, all day. Seek on rocks, sandbanks, pilings; mussels cling to them, or to other mussels, by "byssus threads" or "beards," extruded steel wool–type filaments, very tough. Gather in cleanest, purest water only. Avoid "red tides," common on West Coast in summer, less common East: sudden proliferations of reddish dinoflagellates, micro-organisms making mussels fat, people sick. Red tides monitored by U.S. Coast Guard, U.S. Fish and Wildlife Service. Check.

Check locally. Unposted areas not necessarily safe. Inquire town shellfish warden, if any, re sewage outlets, etc. If license to gather is required, try town hall. Then help self. Recommended equipment: screwdriver or chisel, gloves if sea cold, carrying bag, rinsing bucket. Best harvest only for immediate use. For storage— 2 days at most—refrigerate clumps as is in plastic bag; don't separate or disturb.

Steamed mussels —a delicious, abundant natural resource

*A fresh light colorful meal—quick to prepare
and easy on the budget.*

A Fast Fish Dinner

Menu
For 6 people

Cold Beet and Cucumber Soup
Fingers of Buttered Pumpernickel Bread

❧

Monkfish Tails en Pipérade — Green and red
*   peppers, onions, herbs, and garlic*
Fresh Tomato Fondue (optional)
Sauté of Zucchini & Co.
French Bread

❧

Cream Cheese and Lemon Flan
Cherries, Grapes, Tangerines, or Berries in
*   Season*

❧

Suggested wines:
A strong dry white wine with the fish:
Burgundy, Côtes du Rhône, chardonnay.
You might also serve a sparkling wine or
a gewürztraminer with the dessert.

When a commercial fisherman hauls in his vast nets, all sorts of finny creatures tumble out; of these, many are edible and some, delicious. But only a few kinds ever turn up on ice at the fish store, and it's a shame. Among the missing until fairly recently was monkfish, also called anglerfish, goosefish, allmouth, molligut, and fishing frog; in French it's *lotte* or *baudroie;* in Italian, *rana* or *coda di rospo* (toad's tail); and its Latin name is *Lophius americanus,* for the American species, and *L. piscatorius,* for the European. European cooks consider it a delicacy; because of the great demand, it's expensive there, with much of it imported from our waters. Monkfish is a good resource in these days of inflation and scarcity. What you buy is thick, firm, snowy-white fillets, chunky things you halve or cut into steaks. Monkfish is a cook's delight because it is so adaptable; its firm texture suits it to dishes like bouillabaisse, and its mild flavor can be stepped up with sauces and marinades.

Quickly cooked fish is a shrewd choice for party hosts who will have to be out all day. For this light, attractive meal we chose a cold beet and cucumber soup and a cream cheese and lemon flan, parts of which can be made in advance, and the monkfish is accompanied with a beautiful platter of sliced and quickly sautéed vegetables. The fish is cooked with a *pipérade,* that classic combination of peppers, onions, and garlic; the juices are reduced and added to a fresh tomato sauce (recipe on page 112), making a pretty dish full of flavor. In Europe, monkfish is often mixed with lobster meat, whose flavor and perfume it absorbs, for an effect of vast opulence.

When we decided to cook monkfish for television, we asked our favorite fish purveyor to supply us with a whole one, not an easy trick since fishermen routinely cut off the edible tail (about one-fifth of the total weight) and throw the rest of the fish overboard. But if anyone could procure a whole monkfish it would be he, one of the sons of a whole family of fish dealers. My request made him shout with laughter. But he found us the 25-pounder you see here.

Even in France, these fish are considered so terrifying to behold that dealers never display them. He was half right. Nobody in the studio fainted, but everybody screamed when the incredible monster was wheeled in on a cart. Imagine a tadpole almost the size and shape of a baby grand piano, with strangely elbowlike jointed fins on either side,

no scales, and skin as loose as a puppy's. Where the piano has keys, the fish has spiny teeth angled inward to form a giant bear trap, and more teeth in patches farther back, and still more under its upward-glaring eyes. The fleshy tongue is as big as your hand; the domed roof of the mouth is as hard as steel plating. Three little wands protrude from the top of the head; the tip of the foremost bears a tiny flap of flesh, the "bait," so called because so used. According to Alan Davidson in *Mediterranean Seafood* (Harmondsworth, England: Penguin Books, 1972), the monkfish's "habit is to excavate and settle into a shallow depression on the bottom. By the time sand particles disturbed by this process have drifted down over the angler it is almost invisible. . . ." It waits, motionless except for the "bait" fluttering in the ripples, just above the gaping maw. Any passing fish or diving bird might well think it was a tidbit floating there. Picture the awful scene!

In the stomach of one monkfish, observers found 21 flounders and 1 dogfish, all eaten at one sitting; in another, 7 wild ducks; in another, a sea turtle. Monkfish apparently don't attack swimming humans, but otherwise, as another fish book reports, "nothing edible that strays within reach comes amiss" to this Sidney Greenstreet of the ocean. The enormous mouth makes it possible for the creature to prey on fish almost its own size; one young 26-incher was found to enclose a 23-inch codling.

The book that provides the above riveting facts is a sober-looking, scholarly volume called *Fishes of the Gulf of Maine,* by Henry B. Bigelow and William C. Schroeder (Washington: U.S. Government Printing Office, 1st revision, 1953). My edition is now out of print, but the book has been republished by Harvard University (Cambridge: Harvard Museum of Comparative Zoology, special publication, 1972). My sources at the museum say there's lots of demand for it. Nothing could be a better sign for American cooks than an increased public interest in fish; it points toward an increased variety at the fishmarket.

In this ferocious-looking 25-pound monkfish, only the tail is edible and prized.

Preparations and Marketing

Recommended Equipment:

You can chop the soup vegetables finely by hand, or in a vegetable mill, but a blender or food processor makes it a breeze.

For the fish and its *pipérade,* you need 2 large nonstick frying pans (or 1, if you make the *pipérade* early), and 1 cover of some sort. Another large frying pan, or a wok, is right for the zucchini dish, and a hand-held slicer or *mandoline*—or a very clever knife.

For the flan, I use a flan ring, foil, a baking stone, and a baker's peel or paddle, or a baking sheet, for sliding; but it can be cooked on a baking sheet or even in a pie pan in the usual manner.

Staples to Have on Hand:

Salt
Peppercorns
Sugar
Nutmeg
Italian or Provençal herb mixture
Pure vanilla extract
Horseradish, bottled or grated fresh
Wine vinegar
Olive oil
Chicken broth (1 cup or ¼ L)
Fish broth (1 cup or ¼ L), or more chicken
    broth

Butter
Eggs (4 "large")
Flour
Garlic
Shallots and scallions
Fresh herbs, such as dill, chives, parsley,
    chervil, basil
Yellow onion (1 large)
Carrots (2 or 3 large)
Lemons (2 or more)
Dry white wine or dry white French vermouth

Specific Ingredients for This Menu:

Monkfish fillets (3½ pounds or 1½ kg)
Heavy cream (½ cup or 1 dL)
Sour cream (1 cup or ¼ L, or more)
Cream cheese (8 ounces or 225 g) ▼
Young white turnips (2 or more)
Parsnips (2 or 3)
Zucchini (2 or 3)
Cucumbers (1)
Red bell peppers (2 large) ▼
Green bell peppers (2 large)
Beets (a 1-pound or 453-g can, or 5 large
    fresh) ▼
Beet juice or bottled borscht (1 cup or ¼ L,
    or more)
Chopped walnuts (4 to 5 Tb)
Optional: ingredients for fresh Tomato
    Fondue (page 112)

▶   **Remarks:**

Cream cheese: try to get the fresh kind, with
no additives to glue it up, but plan to use it
within a few days because it contains no
preservatives. However, it freezes successfully, and the thawed cheese is fine for cooking. *Red bell peppers:* if you can't find them
fresh, use canned or bottled pimiento, or tomatoes. *Beets:* if you plan to use fresh ones,
please look at the Post-Postscript of this chapter for hints on their preparation.

Note "bait" on wand protruding from monkfish head.

Cold Beet and Cucumber Soup

With sour cream and dill, and buttered black bread

This is on the idea of a borscht because it is a beet soup. Otherwise it follows no traditions except the taste of its maker. I love fresh beets in season, but am delighted that canned beets have such good flavor and color; I find them excellent here.

For about 6 cups (1 ½ L)

3 or 4 scallions, or 1 or 2 shallots

1 cucumber, peeled and seeded

A 1-pound (453-g) can of beets, whole, sliced, or julienned, or 2 cups (½ L) cooked fresh beets, including some juice

1 cup (¼ L) or more beet juice or bottled borscht

1 cup (¼ L) or more chicken broth, fresh or canned

1 tsp or more horseradish, bottled or grated fresh

1 Tb or so wine vinegar

Salt and pepper to taste

For garnish: 1 cup (¼ L) or more sour cream and a handful of fresh dill sprigs (or chives or parsley)

Equipment:

An electric blender or food processor, or vegetable mill, or wooden bowl and chopper

With an electric blender or food processor, first chop the scallions, then all the rest of the solid ingredients with just enough of the liquids to blend—do not purée too fine; thin out to desired consistency with beet juice and broth; season to taste. Or, if using a vegetable mill, purée solids into a bowl with enough liquid for their passage (by hand, chop solids fine); blend in liquids and flavorings.

Chill several hours. Carefully taste and correct seasoning again, since it may need more after chilling. Serve in individual bowls, and top each portion with a spoonful of sour cream and a sprinkling of dill, chives, or parsley.

🕐 May be made 2 or 3 days in advance of serving; store in a covered container in the refrigerator.

Buttered fingers of pumpernickel bread accompany cool beet and cucumber soup.

Monkfish Tails en Pipérade

Fish steaks simmered in herbs, wine, and red and green peppers

The firm, close-textured lean flesh of the monkfish needs a little extra cooking time to make it tender, and it wants to simmer with flavorful ingredients because it has no pronounced taste of its own. The hearty Basque combination here does the work it should, besides being wonderfully colorful to look at. Incidentally, this also makes a delicious cold fish dish, as noted at the end of the recipe.

For 6 people

The Pipérade Mixture:
2 large green bell peppers

2 large red bell peppers (if you have none, use tomatoes or pimientos as noted in recipe)

1 large yellow onion

2 Tb or so olive oil

2 or 3 cloves garlic, puréed

1 tsp or so mixed herbs, like Italian or Provençal seasoning

¼ tsp or so salt

Freshly ground pepper

The Fish and Other Ingredients:
3½ pounds (1½ kg) trimmed monkfish fillets

Salt, pepper, and flour

2 Tb or so olive oil

About 1 cup (¼ L) each dry white wine or French vermouth, and fish or chicken broth

Fresh tomato fondue (page 112), optional

Equipment:
1 or 2 large frying pans, nonstick recommended

Preliminary cooking of the pipérade vegetables

Wash, halve, stem, and seed the peppers, and cut into very fine long thin slices. (If you have no red peppers, you may use peeled seeded tomatoes, cut into slices and added when the green peppers go over the fish; or use slices of canned red pimiento.) Peel the onion, halve through the root, and cut into thin lengthwise slices. Film a large frying pan with the oil, add the sliced vegetables, and cook over moderate heat for 4 to 5 minutes while you add the garlic, herbs, and seasonings. Vegetables should be partially cooked; they will finish with the fish.

🕐 May be done in advance to this point; let cool uncovered, then transfer to a bowl, cover, and refrigerate.

Preliminary sautéing of the fish

Cut the fish into serving chunks. Just before you are to sauté it, season all sides with a sprinkling of salt and pepper, dredge lightly in

In the unlikely event you catch your own monkfish, here is how to clean it.

Monkfish tail: loose skin cuts and pulls off easily.

Cut closely against each side of single central bone to fillet the fish.

Note firm white flesh of monkfish fillet.

flour, and shake off excess. Into a second frying pan (or in the same one, if you have done the vegetables ahead), pour in enough oil to film it and set over moderately high heat. When very hot but not smoking, add the fish in one layer. Sauté for 2 minutes, then turn and sauté for 2 minutes on the other side—not to brown, merely to stiffen slightly. Spread the cooked vegetables over the fish.

🕐 May be done several hours in advance to this point; let cool uncovered, then cover and refrigerate.

Final cooking
10 minutes or so

Pour in the wine and broth—enough to come halfway up the fish. Cover and simmer about 10 minutes. Fish is done when it has turned from springy to gently soft—it needs a little more cooking than other fish, but must not overcook and fall apart. Arrange fish and vegetables on a hot platter and cover. Rapidly boil down the juices in frying pan until almost syrupy, then spoon them over the fish, and serve, surrounded by the optional tomato fondue.

🕐 Fish can wait, unsauced, 15 minutes or so on its platter; cover and set over a pan of hot water. Boil down the juices separately, drain juices from waiting fish and add to sauce, then spoon sauce over fish just before serving.

Variations on the Sauce—with Cream, or with Aïoli:
Because this menu ends with a cream cheese flan, I did not enrich the cooking juices. Two luscious alternatives, especially if you wish to accompany the fish with plain boiled rice—which goes nicely—are the following:

Cream. When you have boiled down the fish cooking juices until they are almost syrupy, dribble them into a small mixing bowl containing ½ cup (1 dL) heavy cream blended with an egg yolk. Return sauce to the pan and stir over low heat just until thickened lightly but well below the simmer. Pour over the fish and serve.

Aïoli. Another suggestion is to have a mixing bowl ready with 1 cup (¼ L) *aïoli*—thick garlic mayonnaise (page 112). Beat the boiled-down juices by dribbles into the *aïoli*, return to the pan to heat gently for a moment without coming near the simmer, then spoon over the fish and serve.

Monkfish en Pipérade Cold:
This recipe is also very good served cold, but you will need to strengthen the flavors. If you are planning to serve it cold, boil down the juices as described; season them highly with lemon juice, more garlic, salt, pepper, and herbs. Spoon sauce over the warm fish, and then let it cool. Serve with lemon wedges and black olives.

Or beat the juices into an *aïoli* garlic mayonnaise, as described in the preceding variation.

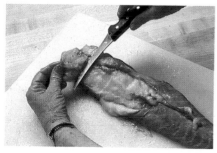

Be sure to cut and peel off grayish membrane covering outer side of fillet, and fish is ready to cook (some markets may not have done this).

After its preliminary sauté, monkfish simmers with wine and pipérade.

Monkfish ready to serve after basting with its concentrated juices

Sauté of Zucchini & Co.

A fast sauté of thinly sliced carrots, turnips, parsnips —and zucchini

Here is a lovely fresh vegetable combination, but while the vegetables may be cut in advance, they can be cooked only at the last moment or they wilt. However, the cooking is a matter of minutes only.

For 6 to 8 people

2 or 3 zucchini
Salt
2 or 3 large carrots
2 or more fine young white turnips
2 or 3 parsnips
2 Tb or more butter
Pepper
Minced fresh green herbs, such as chives, basil, chervil, parsley (optional)

Equipment:

A hand-held vegetable slicer is useful here— a food processor can't do the work neatly enough; a large frying pan or wok

Cut the tips off each end of the zucchini, and scrub but don't peel them; slice very thin crosswise—⅛ inch (½ cm). Toss in a bowl with a good sprinkling of salt, and let drain while preparing the other vegetables. Peel and cut all of them into equally thin rounds.

🕐   Vegetables may be prepared several hours in advance; cover and refrigerate.

Just before serving, heat the butter in a frying pan or wok and add the carrots, turnips, and parsnips, tossing them almost continuously over high heat. Meanwhile, drain the zucchini and dry in paper towels; when the other vegetables are becoming tender, add the zucchini. Toss for 2 or 3 minutes. Vegetables should retain a lightly crunchy texture. Season to taste, toss with a little fresh butter if you wish, and the optional green herbs. Serve at once.

This vegetable sauté is a quick last-minute affair.

Forming Tart Shells in a Flan Ring

An open-faced tart or flan encased in just its shell is always chic. The dough is formed in a bottomless ring that sits upon a baking sheet or, in this case, upon a thin sheet of foil placed upon a baker's peel, or rimless cookie sheet, or anything from which you can slide the flan ring and foil onto an oven baking stone.

Always be sure the dough is well rested and chilled, and work as rapidly as possible so that it will not soften and be difficult to handle. If it does soften, refrigerate everything—dough, flan, baking sheet—let chill for 20 minutes, and then take up where you left off.

Butter the inside of the ring and the foil or baking sheet. Roll out the dough to a thickness of 3/16 inch (scant ¾ cm), and 2 inches (5 cm) larger all around than your flan ring.

Here is how to form the dough (formula is on page 110):

1)Fold the dough in half, and the half in quarters. Set buttered flan ring on buttered foil or baking sheet, and position point of dough in center of ring.

2)Unfold dough and press it lightly against foil or baking sheet, and rest it against edge of ring. Then gently ease and push almost ½ inch (1½ cm) of it down side of ring all around, to make its wall thicker.

3)Fold dough outward from side of ring, and roll pin over top of ring to cut off the excess dough.

4)Gently push the dough lining up from the edge all around ring, to make it stand about ⅜ inch (1 cm) above rim.

5)Press a decorative pattern all around top rim of dough with the back of a knife.

6)Prick bottom of dough, going just down through to foil or baking sheet, with a sharp-pronged fork to make tiny holes that will prevent pastry from rising during baking.

Cream Cheese and Lemon Flan

A cheesecake tart

This combination has more texture than a plain custard, and is moister than most cheesecakes I have known. I like it served slightly warm, or at room temperature, although it is good cold, too.

Manufacturing Note:

There is no requirement that you bake the flan on a pizza stone, as illustrated here. Form and bake it in a ring set on a pastry sheet, or in a pie tin, or use a frozen pie shell, or no pastry shell at all—just a baking dish. I developed the pizza stone system because I use one for baking French bread, pizzas, and pita breads; its hot surface gives a crisp brown crust without your having to prebake the shell before you fill it. No soggy bottom!

For a 10-inch (25-cm) flan, serving 10

A 10-inch (25-cm) dough-lined flan ring set on buttered foil (see manufacturing note above, and alternatives at end of recipe.

The Cream Cheese and Lemon Filling:
About 2 ½ cups (6 dL)

4 "large" eggs

¼ tsp salt

½ cup (1 dL) heavy cream

The grated rind of 1 lemon

4 Tb fresh lemon juice (or more if you like a very lemony flavor)

8 ounces (225 g) cream cheese, preferably fresh

4 Tb sugar

A pinch of nutmeg

1 tsp pure vanilla extract

For Top Decoration During Baking:

4 to 5 Tb each sugar and chopped walnuts

Equipment:

A pizza stone or oven griddle and baker's peel or a baking sheet; an electric blender or food processor is useful for the filling, or a vegetable mill or sieve and wire whip

Prepare the pastry dough in the flan ring and chill for 20 minutes. Meanwhile, either whisk up all the filling ingredients in a blender or food processor, or purée the cream cheese through a vegetable mill or sieve, and beat in the rest of the items with a wire whip.

🕐 Both dough-lined ring and filling may be prepared hours in advance; cover each and refrigerate.

Either Baking on an Oven Stone:
*30 to 35 minutes at 425–350°F/
220–180°C*

Set pizza stone or oven griddle on a rack in the middle level of the oven and preheat oven for 15 to 20 minutes to be sure stone is really hot. Then slide out oven rack, slide flan and foil onto stone (1), and pour in the filling to within ⅛ inch (½ cm) of rim (2). (Do not overfill or you risk spillage during baking.)

Bake for 10 minutes, or just until filling has set a little; spread the sugar and walnut mixture over the surface (3). Bake another 10

minutes, then lower oven temperature to 350°F/180°C. Flan is done when it has puffed and browned lightly, and when bottom of crust has browned—30 to 35 minutes in all.

Serving
Remove flan from oven, let settle 5 minutes, then, with flan ring still in place, slide off foil onto a rack. Let cool to tepid before serving. Or serve it cold.

🕐 Flan is at its best when freshly cooked, but you may cover and refrigerate the leftovers, and serve flan cold or rewarmed the next day.

Or Baking in the Conventional Way:
I do think that if you are cooking a tart, quiche, or flan in a pie tin or in a ring set on a baking sheet, you are wise to precook the pastry before filling it. This will prevent the crust from being uncooked or partially cooked on the bottom. To do so, simply line the pricked raw dough-filled form with lightweight buttered foil, fill with dried beans or rice (which you keep on hand for this purpose), and bake at 400°F/205°C for 10 minutes, or until when you lift the foil you see the pastry has set. Then remove foil and beans, prick lightly again, and continue baking for 5 minutes or more until dough is just beginning to color and just starting to shrink from sides of mold. Then pour in the filling, and proceed to bake as in the preceding recipe.

🕐 Partially baked pastry shells may be frozen.

⏱ *Timing*

You'll need to be at the stove for about 7 to 8 minutes to cook the sautéed vegetables. If you don't want to spend that much time between courses, leave the root vegetables a bit underdone off heat, while you're having your soup; then add the zucchini and give the mixture a careful 2 to 3 minutes' sauté before serving it. Final cooking of the monkfish takes only 10 minutes, and can be done along with the vegetables or a few minutes earlier, since this dish can wait a little.

Otherwise, you have no problems at all. The soup, the *pipérade,* tomato sauce, and the pastry dough and filling for the flan can be made the day before your party; then you assemble and bake the flan late in the afternoon on the "day of." At that time you would cut the vegetables, while the flan bakes. Or you could make and freeze the *pipérade* and the flan dough far in advance.

In short, if you possess a food processor, this very festive meal can be executed in less than an hour's working time, comfortably broken into short bouts.

Menu Variations

Other cold *soup* recipes are discussed in "Picnic," page 93. There are many possible versions for beet soup and borscht.

Other firm lean white *fish* that can be cut into steaks are conger eel, cusk, and halibut. See also skate wings in black butter and caper sauce, in the Postscript. Tuna (or swordfish, which I much prefer) is good in *pipérade* or braised with lettuce, herbs, and wine (in *J.C.'s Kitchen*), or you could use bluefish. For other ways of cooking monkfish, see farther on.

This would make a wonderful summer meal, but you'd need to suit your *vegetables* to the season—zucchini, carrots, and cucumbers, for instance. The wok sauté of spinach and zucchini on page 10 is a summery thought.

A lemon *dessert* is a natural for a fish dinner. There are other lemon tarts (or flans) in *Mastering I* and *J.C.'s Kitchen;* if you want to make this light meal still lighter, what about a sherbet? Or, in between, a lemon soufflé?

And now for more monkfish!

Lotte à l'Américaine

Monkfish steaks with wine and tomato sauce

This is a splendid combination, and one that though usually associated with lobsters is also traditional in France with monkfish. Start out in exactly the same way as in the original recipe, seasoning, flouring, and sautéing the fish steaks in oil. When the time is up you may, if you feel flush, pour in ¼ cup (½ dL) Cognac, let it bubble, then ignite it with a lighted match. Flame it away a few seconds, then douse it with the white wine or vermouth. Add the sautéed onion, and garlic, but instead of peppers use tomatoes—spread on and around the fish 2 cups (½ L) fresh tomato pulp and 2 tablespoons tomato paste. Use ½ teaspoon tarragon instead of mixed herbs. Cover and simmer 10 minutes, then remove the fish to a platter, boil down the sauce to thicken it, taste carefully for seasoning, spoon over the fish, decorate with parsley, and serve.

Broiled Monkfish

Since monkfish has no distinctive flavor of its own, I find it needs assistance when it is baked or broiled. I've had good success slicing a large fillet in half horizontally, so it will not be more than about ¾ inch (2 cm) thick. Then I paint it with a mixture of puréed garlic, salt, lemon juice, oil, and thyme, rosemary, oregano, or an herb mixture, and let it marinate for an hour or more before cooking it. I then like to sprinkle the top with a little paprika, broil it close to the heating element for 5 minutes or so, and bake at 400°F/205°C for another 10 minutes, basting it with a little white wine or vermouth.

Leftovers

The *soup*, since it keeps for several days refrigerated, is a good recipe to double. I think it loses a bit of its keen flavor if heated, but you might prefer it that way.

The *fish* dish is just as good cold as hot. If you bought extra monkfish, the recipe has variants, and there are two more in Menu Variations. As for *pipérade,* it is a splendid kitchen staple. Here in our recipe it is not fully cooked when it goes over the fish, but while you are at it you could double the amount of vegetables in the pan initially, use half for the fish, and continue cooking the rest until the vegetables are just tender. Then you can bottle and refrigerate or freeze it, and use it, for instance, to garnish an open-faced omelet, or bake it in the egg and cheese mixture for a quiche, or serve it as an accompaniment to pasta, hamburgers, steak, broiled fish, or chicken. It's wonderful to have a quick ready-made garnish on hand to dress up otherwise simple dishes.

The *vegetable* sauté is not reheatable, but it's fine in a soup.

Refrigerate the delicious *flan,* which is nice cold, and will keep for several days.

Postscript: Another odd fish

It's odd enough that a squash should behave like spaghetti, but how about a fish? When you eat skate, you don't just cut down through it; you draw your knife horizontally over the flesh, which promptly separates into long juicy white strands, slightly gelatinous and of the most delicate flavor. In Europe, it's tremendously popular, and savvy fish cooks here have always served it, but it should be more widely known. Especially so since skate are profuse in our waters—hideous creatures, cousins to the devil-fish and the manta ray. The barn-door skate's flat diamond-shaped body is often 5 feet (1½ meters) long, but you'll rarely see a whole one. Only the wings, or side fins, of skate are eaten, and those generally sold weigh from 1½ pounds (675 g) each untrimmed. Several varieties, all very similar, are marketed here.

A story which keeps turning up in cookbooks is that skate wings are often cut into rounds and sold as scallops, or "mock scallops." It seemed unlikely to me, since scallop flesh is grained vertically, and skate horizontally—moreover, skate meat separates so readily when cooked. But I checked with two experts. George Berkowitz said that, in his 30 years' experience in the fish business, he'd never seen it done. Bob Learson, of the National Marine Fisheries laboratory in Gloucester, Massachusetts, pointed out that the way cartilage is distributed in a skate wing would make the process impractical on a commercial scale. Both men dismiss the scallop story as an old wives' tale.

If you go fishing for skate, you'll have fun. They'll bite at any bait and fight like fury.

Having caught a skate or bought a piece of one, you give it special treatment. The skin is covered with a gluey wet film that should smell very fresh, not at all ammoniac, and you remove this by washing the wing in several waters. It should then be refrigerated overnight in water. My favorite way of cooking skate is to be found in a French classic, *La Cuisine de*

Madame Saint-Ange (Paris: Larousse, 1958; now out of print, but there is a Swiss edition). Cook the wings of all skate the same way and for the same length of time, as their thickness doesn't vary with their breadth. Cut off the thin, finny, outer-fringe part of the wing with scissors, discard it, and lay the remainder in a high-sided pan like a chicken fryer, cover by at least ½ inch (1½ cm) with cold water, adding 5 tablespoons wine vinegar per quart (or liter), with 1 tablespoon salt, a small onion sliced thin, an imported bay leaf, a pinch of thyme, and 8 to 10 parsley stems. Bring just to the boil, turn down heat, cover, and let poach below the simmer for exactly 25 minutes. Carefully scrape the skin from each piece (it comes off easily), and return to the poaching water until you are ready to serve. I like it best with black butter sauce. For black butter, heat butter until it begins to turn medium brown; remove it from the heat and toss in a spoonful of capers. Sprinkle chopped fresh parsley over the skate, and watch it bubble as you pour over it the hot butter sauce. A wonderful dish.

Post-Postscript: Fresh beets

Fresh beets, with their dusty ruby-purple bulbs and dark-green leaves that are ribbed in red, are available every month of the year but appear abundantly in most markets only between May and October. I must admit to quite a passion for fresh beets, with their full-bodied taste and hearty color. I feel I am eating something really worthwhile in the vegetable line, and indeed I am because beets are full of vitamins and minerals as well as flavor. As a matter of fact, plain cooked fresh beets are great food for dieters just because they are so nourishing, and they can be eaten as is, with no butter or oil or cream to fatten your calorie count. Thumbing through my handful of vegetarian cookbooks, by the way, I find among them no interest in beets.

Why, when beets have so much going for them in every way?

Anyone who has lived in France remembers the large cooked beets at the vegetable stalls in the markets. You peel them, slice them into a vinaigrette with minced shallots, and surround them with watercress or *mâche* (corn salad, or lamb's lettuce, or *Valerianella olitoria,* which grows wild in this country but is cultivated as a salad plant in Europe). The beets you buy in France have been cooked in an oven, and they are much larger and probably older than ours because they presumably bake for 6 to 8 hours. In an old French book I consulted, I read that one should put the beets on a bed of wet straw, cover them with an upside-down earthenware bowl, and bake them until the skins are shriveled and even charred. The straw and the charring must give French beets their very special taste. (My book doesn't tell me what size of beet, nor what temperature of oven, but I have heard they used to be cooked in bakers' big ovens, after the bread for the day was done. It must, then, have been in a slow oven.)

Fresh beets can be boiled, baked, steamed, or pressure-cooked. I like boiling the least because you lose color and, I think, a bit of flavor. Baking takes too long—2½ to 3 hours in a slow oven. Steaming works well, and the beets are done in about 40 to 45 minutes. Pressure cooking is my choice because it takes but 20 minutes, there is little loss of color, and the flavor is fine. I did not, by the way, find that baked beets had better flavor than steamed or pressure-cooked beets, but I had them in a covered casserole at 275°F/135°C along with a sample batch of individual beets wrapped in foil—had no straw on hand!

To prepare beets for cooking
Cut off the stems about 1½ inches (4 cm) above the tops of the beets, snip off their tails about ¼ inch (¾ cm) below the bottoms, and be sure the bulbs of the beets are whole and unblemished—a bit of stem and a tight skin will prevent the vivid color and vital juices from escaping too much during cooking. Brush the beets clean under cold water.

Steamed Fresh Beets:

For young beets about 2 inches (5 cm) in diameter

Place prepared beets in a vegetable steamer or on a rack in a saucepan with 1 inch (2½ cm) or so of water, cover tightly, and steam 40 minutes, or until beets feel tender when pierced with a small knife, and peel loosens easily.

Pressure-cooked Beets:

For 2-inch (5-cm) beets

Place beets on rack in pressure cooker with ½ inch (1½ cm) water, and bring to full pressure. Cook for 20 minutes, then release pressure. (Somewhat smaller and somewhat larger beets will take the same amount of time, and slight overcooking seems to do little harm.)

Some Ideas for Hot Fresh Beets:

Slice off the stem ends, peel the beets, and they are ready to serve in any way you choose. The simplest and one of the best ways is that of quartering or slicing them, then tossing in butter, salt, pepper, and perhaps a sprinkling of minced shallots or scallions, and parsley or chives. Serve them with chops, steaks, hamburgers, broiled fish, or broiled chicken.

Beets Gratinéed with Cheese:

Here is certainly one of the most delicious ways to serve hot beets, and especially recommended if you are having a meatless meal because beets and cheese make a full and almost meaty combination. The only drawback is looks—purply red plus the brown-yellow of the baked cheese—and I don't know how you get around that except to revel in the flavor.

Warm the cooked sliced or quartered beets in butter, salt, pepper, and a sprinkling of minced shallots or scallions, then simmer for 5 minutes or so with spoonfuls of heavy cream (a spoonful per beet would be ample). Arrange in layers in a shallow baking dish with a good sprinkling of cheese, either Parmesan alone or a mixture, and spread grated cheese over the top. Shortly before serving, set under a moderately hot broiler to let slowly heat through until bubbling, and the cheese has browned lightly on top.

These would go nicely with eggs, or broiled meats, fish, or chicken, or could be a separate course.

Some Ideas for Cold Fresh Cooked Beets:

Slice off the stem ends, peel the beets, and slice, quarter, dice, or julienne them. Simply toss them in a vinaigrette dressing, decorate with minced parsley and/or chives, and serve them alone, or with watercress or other greens, or with cold string beans, or with potato salad—but do not mix them with other ingredients until the last minute unless you want everything to be stained purple beet color. Serve as a first course, or with hardboiled eggs, cold fish, or cold cuts.

Or serve them with a sour cream or yogurt dressing—blend into either one prepared mustard and horseradish to taste, season with salt and pepper, and spoon into a serving dish; arrange the beets on top, and decorate with parsley. Serve as a salad course or first course, or to accompany broiled or boiled fish or chicken.

Beet Greens—Beet Leaves:

The fresh leaves from a bunch of young beets make a fine green vegetable. Remove leaves from stems, cut leaves into chiffonade, very thin strips, and sauté in a frying pan or wok—like kale or collards or turnip greens. I tried blanching beet greens, and found that the green color held up beautifully but the flavor was far less interesting than the plain sauté.

To Get Beet Juice Off Your Hands, Etc.:

Rinse your hands in cold water, then rub table salt over them; wash in cold soap and water, then in warm soap and water. (Salt helps to remove the red color—just as salt on a red-wine spill will speed the washing.) Fingernails are another matter—I scrub them, then use cuticle remover solution, and scrub again. Use household bleach on your work surfaces for stubborn beet stains.

*Take it along in your Rolls, or your Volks;
the ritziest portable feast imaginable.*

Picnic

Menu
For 8 or more people

Gazpacho Salad —Layers of colorful freshly cut vegetables with bread crumbs and garlic dressing in a cylindrical glass bowl

❧

Fish Terrine, Straight Wharf Restaurant —A tri-color mousse of sole and scallops with watercress and salmon

❧

Pâté en Croûte —Spiced and wine-flavored ground meats baked in a decorative pastry crust

❧

A selection of accompaniments —Carrot sticks, cauliflowerettes, and olives, as well as rare mustards and pickles

❧

A variety of fine fresh breads —French, sourdough rye both light and dark, and whole-grain loaves

❧

A platter of cheeses, and bunches of grapes

❧

Plantation Spice Cookies

❧

Suggested drinks:
Chilled dry white wine (riesling, Muscadet, Chablis, or chardonnay), and a picnic red — Beaujolais or zinfandel; beer; iced tea; selected soft drinks; a large thermos of hot coffee

The best picnic I've ever read of was given during World War II by an Englishman of legendary courage, the Duke of Suffolk. This black-bearded daredevil had recruited and trained a squad of volunteers for the most blood-chilling of all wartime duties, the defusing of live bombs. Having been called down to one of the Channel ports after a Nazi air raid, the duke and his men, tense and exhausted, were returning to London after a grisly day on the docks. Suddenly, on a muddy road in what must have seemed the middle of nowhere, Suffolk signaled the truck convoy to stop. He then blew a whistle and lo, out from behind a hedge purred his Rolls-Royce, laden with hampers, crystal, silver, damask, and a butler who unpacked and served a noble feast. Unbeknownst to the men, their road home passed close to Suffolk's country seat.

It wouldn't have been possible, in those lean and rationed years, to offer the meal we're having today —although, goodness knows, no picnickers ever deserved it more than the bomb squad. But at any rate the party possessed the three characteristics I most enjoy at a good picnic: surprise, luxury, and plenty. It's not worthwhile eating too much —which you can't help doing outdoors —unless the food is marvelous. In our family, we all love hard-boiled eggs and tuna fish sandwiches. But that's not picnicking, that's brown bagging, something we all do once in a while when we're too busy to fix ourselves a fine lunch.

Paper plates and plastic forks have their place —in a brown bag. At a real picnic I like real cutlery, but don't of course insist on damask and porcelain. Our bright plastic plates travel nicely, as does every dish on the menu ... the *pâté en croûte* snug in its mold, and the fish mousse in its thick-walled, chill-conserving terrine. For the gazpacho salad, we have used a straight-sided glass bowl, to show off the rainbow layers of vegetables. The whole works goes into insulated chests—how did we ever manage without?

Gazpacho in its primal state is a soup. But why not keep the gazpacho idea and serve it in a compact form? As a soup, gazpacho is an ancient dish, mentioned in both Old and New Testaments, and known in early Greece and Rome. Nowadays, however, most of us associate it with Spain, especially with the hot climate and searing summer sun of Andalusia, and in particular with the city of Seville. As with cassoulet and bouillabaisse, and even with our own Indian puddings and fish chowders, there are dozens of versions. Some thirty classic gazpachos exist, according to Barbara Norman in her *Spanish Cookbook* (New York: Atheneum, 1966). And there are variations on the thirty, she notes; a gazpacho can be thick or liquid, it can be served at any time during the meal, and rather than the traditional tomato red, it can even be white—when made with olive oil, garlic, and almonds. Alice B. Toklas, after the death of her friend Gertrude Stein, made a sort of gazpacho-quest of an Andalusian tour, and although she ate some marvelous examples, she could find no historical information on the subject in Spain itself. According to her lively account in *The Alice B. Toklas Cookbook* (New York: Harper, 1954), one clerk at a bookstore said to her, "Oh, gazpachos are only eaten in Spain by peasants and Americans." A final quote on the matter comes from M. F. K. Fisher, in *The Art of Eating* (New York: Vintage, 1976): "Above all it should be tantalizing, fresh, and faintly perverse as are all primitive dishes eaten by worldly people."

The word "gazpacho," it says in *The Cooking of Spain and Portugal* (New York: Time-Life Books, 1969), comes from the Arabic, and means soaked bread. And indeed bread appears in almost every version one runs into. Bread was much employed in the recipes of yore, not only as a thickener and nourisher, but simply so as not to waste a crumb.

Bread crumbs appear again in this meal, in the fish terrine—but I have no qualms about it because in the two dishes the taste and effect are so different that the crumbs become just another staple element, like salt. (Just be sure to get very good bread with body. Soft, squashy white bread will disintegrate.) A few years ago, the fish terrine would have been an unthinkable luxury at any but a princely picnic, because it took hours to purée the fish finely, pounding it in a mortar, sieving it, and finally adding cream, almost drop by drop. Even now, like the duke's crystal and silver in a brambly English lane, a fish mousse lends a note of slightly incongruous finesse, which I vastly enjoy, to an outdoor meal. It has a lovely texture; the flavor is unique, and suave to a degree, and the colors make one think of a subtle French painting—ivory-white, pearl-pink, and the green you sometimes see just after sunset. Celestial—and with a food processor, almost shockingly easy to do.

Equally luxurious, but in a quite opposite way—a portly burgher versus a court lady—is the hearty, handsome, porkily perfumed *pâté en croûte.* To call it a meat loaf baked in dough is true to the letter but not the spirit. Its rich meat laced with Port and brandy, spices, and herbs, its darkly gleaming aspic layer, and its greatcoat of heavy pastry, decorated fatly and fancifully—a traditional folk art—it is always the *pièce de résistance* on a table. Molds come in many shapes, but I find our corset-waisted one especially amusing. Set about with cheeses and big fresh country loaves, and grapes and bottles of wine, it looks almost pompously self-satisfied.

We wind up our feast with a delightful old-fashioned sort of cookie, a spice-ball variation containing peanuts, with the aroma of spices and dark molasses. Making these big savory cookies is easy, and children love to do it. The old meaning of the word "picnic" is a party to which everyone contributes, and I've purposely chosen every dish on our menu to be something one could easily carry to a friend's party as a welcome gift. If the children make the cookies, have them double the recipe, or they'll all disappear on the way.

Preparations and Marketing

Recommended Equipment:
A mincing meal indeed! Of course you can do it all by hand, but it's light work if you have a food processor for making bread crumbs and puréeing the fish for the terrine. A heavy-duty electric mixer with a flat beating blade is fine for both the crust and the filling of your *pâté en croûte*. Either a processor or a mixer will help with the cookie dough.

The gazpacho, however, demands good knifework: paring knives for trimming the vegetables and a very sharp French knife for mincing them and dicing them. You'll need 3 or 4 mixing bowls and 3 large sieves, and a 2-quart (2-L) cylindrical glass bowl is ideal for showing off your handiwork.

The mousse recipe was designed for a 5- to 6-cup (1¼- to 1½-L) terrine or loaf pan for baking and serving. (The mousse and its stripes could be adapted to a melon mold, however.)

A special spring-form mold, hinged and latched for easy removal, is ideal for baking *pâté en croûte;* the mold can be had at fancy cookware shops and comes in a variety of shapes. If you can't find one, don't be deterred; see recipe for other possibilities. You do need a pastry brush for glazing, and a bulb baster.

To chop peanuts for the cookies: blenders and processors won't work on the peanut shape. A nut chopper or grater is best, or a wooden bowl and an old-fashioned hand chopper. Have several baking sheets, since the recipe is for 24 cookies, and each sheet will take only 9.

Staples to Have on Hand:

Salt
White and black peppercorns
Sugar
Powdered cloves, cinnamon, nutmeg, allspice,
    and ginger
Ground imported bay leaves
Ground thyme
Fresh basil leaves, or dried oregano
Hot pepper sauce
Prepared Dijon-type mustard
Dark unsulphured molasses
Red-wine vinegar
Prepared horseradish
Optional: capers, olives, anchovies
Baking soda
Gelatin (4 Tb or 4 packages)
Unsalted butter
Olive oil
Lard
French- or Italian-style bread (½ loaf)
Garlic
Lemons (2)
Scallions
Optional: shallots
Parsley; basil and chives if available

Specific Ingredients for This Menu:

Lox or smoked salmon (¼ pound or 115 g)
Fillets of white fish (1½ pounds or 675 g)
Scallops (½ pound or 225 g)
Ground veal (1½ pounds or 675 g)
Ground lean pork (1½ pounds or 675 g)
Ground fresh pork fat (1 pound or 450 g)
For optional pâté garnish: chicken livers, or
    boiled ham for dice or strips, or veal for
    strips, and/or truffles, or pistachio nuts,
    or your own choice (1 cup or ¼ L)
Optional: pig's caul (1 sheet) or strips of fresh
    pork fat ⅛ inch (½ cm) thick (about 1
    pound or 450 g)
Best-quality clarified brown stock (page 66), or
    canned consommé (4 cups or 1 L)
Cucumbers (2 or 3)
Green bell peppers (2 or 3)
Red bell peppers (2 or 3), or red pimiento
Mild red onion (1 large)
Avocados (2 or 3), ripe and firm
Onions (4 to 6 medium)

Fresh tomato pulp (3 cups or ¾ L; 12
    tomatoes), and/or canned Italian
    tomatoes
Celery (2 or 3 stalks)
Watercress (1 large bunch)
Heavy cream (3½ cups, or 8 dL)
Sour cream (1 cup or ¼ L)
Unbleached all-purpose flour (7½ cups; 2
    pounds, 3 ounces, or 1 kg)
Eggs (1½ dozen "large")
Unsalted peanuts (1 cup or ¼ L)
Cognac or Armagnac; dry Port wine
Additional items as you wish: raw vegetable
    snacks, pickles, olives, mustards, grapes,
    cheeses, breads

▶   ### Remarks:

Fish fillets: you can choose among sole, flounder, conger eel, tilefish, petrale sole, monkfish, and halibut. *Scallops:* even more perishable than fin fish, these should ideally be used the day you buy them. Sniff them in the market to be sure they're very fresh. *Fresh pork shoulder butt* has the correct proportion of fat to lean; buy a 2½-pound (1350-g) piece. *Pig's caul:* you don't have to have it, but if you want to use it, you may have to special-order this unless you live in a neighborhood that makes sausage cakes and caters to a European trade. It is the lining of the pig's visceral cavity, and every porker has one: a thin membrane streaked with cobwebby lines of fat that serves as an edible wrapping in sausage making, or for holding stuffing or flavoring around meat or poultry, or for lining pâté crusts. If more of us demanded pig's caul from our markets, we'd find it there. It freezes nicely, too. For pig's caul, substitute strips of *fresh pork fat:* this also may be hard to get. I generally trim mine from pork roasts, and freeze it. If the strips are too thick, cover them with wax paper and pound them with a rubber hammer, bottle, or whatever. If you can't get fresh pork fat, blanch bacon strips in a large pot of boiling water for 10 minutes.

Gazpacho Salad

Layers of diced peppers, onions, celery, cucumbers, avocados, and tomatoes interspersed with fresh bread crumbs and an herbal oil and garlic dressing

All the refreshing flavors of a gazpacho, but rather than being a soup it has become a mixed raw vegetable accompaniment to picnic food—a crudité combo in a pretty bowl. And it is equally delicious on any summer table with cold meats or fish, or with poached or scrambled eggs.

Manufacturing Note:

There is lots of dicing here—good practice—and it is far more attractive done evenly by hand than roughly by machine. Cut and flavor each item separately, and you want the tomatoes and cucumbers to drain well before they go into their final phase or they will exude so much water you will have soup rather than salad.

For 2 quarts (2 L), serving 8 or more

The Vegetables and Bread Crumbs:

3 cups (¾ L) tomato pulp—fresh in season or a combination of fresh and canned Italian plum tomatoes (see directions in recipe)

Salt and red-wine vinegar as needed

2 or 3 cucumbers

¼ tsp sugar

2 or 3 each green bell peppers and red bell peppers (or, lacking red peppers, use a jar or so of canned red pimiento)

1 large mild red onion

2 or 3 celery stalks

About 2 cups (½ L) lightly pressed down, fresh crumbs from crustless nonsweet French- or Italian-style white bread (see directions in recipe)

The Herbal Oil and Garlic Dressing:

2 or 3 large cloves garlic

1 tsp salt, more if needed

Zest (yellow part of peel) of ½ lemon

Herbs: fresh basil leaves most desirable, otherwise fragrant dried oregano, or another of your choice

2 tsp prepared Dijon-type mustard

2 to 3 Tb lemon juice

½ cup (1 dL) or so good olive oil

Wine vinegar if needed

Freshly ground pepper and drops of hot pepper sauce

Other Ingredients:

2 or 3 ripe firm avocados

2 or 3 minced shallots or scallions

4 to 5 Tb fresh minced parsley

Capers, olives, anchovies for final decoration (optional)

Equipment:

3 sieves; 3 or 4 medium mixing bowls; a medium mortar and pestle, or heavy bowl and a masher of some sort (wooden spoon); a blender or food processor for making the bread crumbs; an attractive glass bowl of about 2 quarts (2 L) to hold the layered gazpacho

The tomatoes

Peel, seed, and juice the tomatoes, and cut into neat dice about ¼-inch (¾-cm) size. Out of season, include a judicious amount of canned peeled Italian-style plum tomatoes—halve

Gazpacho salad

them, scoop out seeds with your fingers, and dice the flesh; they are usually rather soft, but they add color and flavor. Fold together in a bowl with about ½ teaspoon salt and 1 teaspoon or so of wine vinegar, let stand 5 minutes, then turn into a sieve set over a bowl to drain while you continue.

The cucumbers

Peel the cucumbers, cut in half lengthwise, and scoop out their seeds by drawing a teaspoon down their lengths. Cut into strips, then into dice about the same size as the tomatoes. Toss in a bowl with 1 tablespoon wine vinegar, ½ teaspoon salt, and ¼ teaspoon sugar. Let stand 5 minutes, then turn into a sieve set over a bowl to drain.

The peppers, onions, and celery

Halve the peppers, remove their seeds and stems, dice the flesh the same size as the tomatoes, and place in a bowl. Peel and dice the red onion (you should have about ⅔ cup or 1½ dL), drop for 15 seconds in a pan of boiling water to remove strong bite, drain, rinse in cold water, and drain again; add to the peppers. Dice the celery, add to the peppers, and then toss the three vegetables together with salt and drops of wine vinegar to taste. Set aside.

The bread crumbs

Cut off crusts, tear bread into smallish pieces, and crumb a handful at a time in a blender or food processor.

The herbal oil and garlic dressing

Peel the garlic cloves, chop fine (or purée through a garlic press), and then pound in the mortar or bowl with 1 teaspoon salt until the consistency of a paste. Mince the lemon zest, add to the mortar, and pound until puréed, then add and pound the herb into the purée. Beat in the mustard with a small wire whip, then the lemon juice, and finally, by droplets, the oil—hoping for a homogenized sauce (but no matter if elements do not cream together: beat up before each use). Season well with more salt, drops of vinegar if needed, pepper, and hot pepper sauce to taste.

The avocados

Halve, seed, peel, and dice the avocados. Rinse in cold water to prevent discoloration, and set aside.

Arranging the gazpacho salad

4 to 6 hours before serving

Be sure the tomatoes are well drained; toss the cucumbers and the pepper-onion mixture in paper towels to dehumidify. The ingredients are to be spread in layers, to make an attractive design when you look through the glass; I shall specify 3 layers here.

Spread ¼ of the crumbs evenly in the bottom of the bowl, cover with ⅓ of the pepper-onion mixture, then ⅓ of the avocados, ⅓ the tomatoes, ⅓ of the cucumbers, then ¼ of the dressing. Continue with crumbs, pepper-onion mixture, avocados, tomatoes, cucumbers, dressing, and so on, ending with a layer of crumbs, then the remaining sauce. Toss the shallots and parsley together and spread over the top. Cover closely with plastic wrap and refrigerate. Just before serving, decorate with capers, olives, and anchovies, if you wish.

🕐   Once the vegetables are prepared, arrange the salad in its bowl so that the ingredients may commune together to make an interesting whole. Leftovers are still good the next day, or may be ground up in a blender or food processor (or stirred together) with tomato juice to make a gazpacho soup . . . in which you might include the preliminary vegetable drainings, which are full of flavor.

Neat knifework makes all the difference in the beauty and taste of a gazpacho salad.

Fish Terrine, Straight Wharf Restaurant— Terrine de Sole aux Trois Mousses

Mousse of sole and scallops layered with watercress and salmon

Here is a lovely terrine indeed, an ivory mousse of sole and scallops puréed together with cream and eggs, interlaced with strips of green watercress and of pink salmon. Serve it hot as a first course or for a luncheon dish, or take it cold, in its terrine or baking dish, on a picnic.

Note: A fish terrine—or pâté—is almost invariably a purée of raw fish that is bound together with eggs, and made light and, in fact, mousselike, with cream. Sometimes the fish mousse stands alone, having enough bodily gelatin and strength to need no other base. This always sounds stylish, but I like a panade (thick cream sauce or bread crumbs) in my mousses and I particularly like the use of fresh bread crumbs here; they absorb the fish juices that would otherwise exude in a sometimes distressing quantity.

Before deciding on this particular mousse, our cooking team tried out quite a number of others. I had myself worked on numerous versions of a scallop mousse and found that it was either rubbery when it had no panade, or it was lacking in scallop flavor when it did. Chef Sara and I tried a mousse of scallops and sole with cream and gelatin that had a delicious flavor—but the unappealing texture of fish gelatin pudding. Finally chef Marion suggested we try her fish terrine, the one she does in Nantucket, where she is summer chef at the Straight Wharf Restaurant. We all liked hers

immensely and this, with one or two jointly arrived-at modifications, is it.

Manufacturing Note—Molded Mousse:
The recipe here is for a fish mousse served directly from its terrine or baking dish, since that is great for a picnic or a covered-dish party. If you want to serve it unmolded, however, just line the inside of the terrine with buttered wax paper, and the mousse will come out easily after it has baked.

For a 5-cup (1¼-L) terrine or bread pan, serving 8 to 10 people

The Garnish—Watercress and Salmon:

1 large bunch fresh watercress
4 or 5 scallions
2½ to 3 Tb butter
¼ pound (115 g) excellent lox or lightly smoked salmon

Fresh fish is essential for a fine terrine—let your nose be the judge.

For the Fish Mousse:

1½ pounds (675 g) of the finest, freshest-smelling fillets of sole or flounder (or other lean white fish such as conger eel, tilefish, petrale sole, monkfish, halibut)

½ pound (225 g) of the freshest-smelling scallops, washed rapidly and drained

2 "large" eggs

1 Tb (or a bit less) salt

2 cups (½ L) lightly pressed down crumbs from crustless nonsweet French- or Italian-style white bread (see gazpacho recipe for directions)

2 to 3 cups (½ to ¾ L) heavy cream

4 Tb fresh lemon juice

Freshly grated white pepper

A speck or so of nutmeg

Equipment:

A food processor; a 5- to 6-cup (1¼- to 1½-L) terrine or loaf pan; several rubber spatulas and soup spoons (useful); 2 or 3 medium mixing bowls; an instant (microwave) meat thermometer (useful)

Preliminaries

Preheat oven to 350° F/180° C and place a roasting pan half full of water in it, for baking the terrine. Cut a piece of wax paper a little larger all around than the terrine, and a piece of aluminum foil slightly larger than that. Butter one side of the wax paper.

Pull the tender leaves and top stems off the watercress (you may save the rest for watercress soup), and chop them into very fine mince with the white and tender green of the scallions; sauté slowly in 2 tablespoons butter for a minute or so, until limp. Set aside in a bowl. Look over the salmon to be sure there are no bones or other debris.

The fish mousse

(If you have a processor with a small container, divide the mousse ingredients in half and do in 2 parts, then beat together in a bowl to blend.)

Cut the fillets into 2-inch (5-cm) pieces and purée with the scallops, using the steel blade. Remove cover and add the eggs, salt, bread crumbs, 2 cups (½ L) cream, the lemon juice, 10 grinds of pepper, and nutmeg. Purée for 30 seconds or so. Remove cover; scrape and stir contents about, and purée longer if not smooth. When you spoon a little up, mousse should hold its shape softly—if you think it could take more cream, start the machine again, and add more in a thin stream, checking that you have not softened the purée too much. Remove cover, and taste carefully for seasoning—it should seem a little oversalted and overseasoned if you are to serve it cold, since the seasonings will become less strong once a mousse is cooked and cooled.

Assembling the terrine

(The mousse is arranged in layers in the terrine: plain mousse, green, plain mousse, salmon, ending with plain mousse. Some of the plain mousse is blended with the watercress and with the salmon; otherwise the layers would separate when the mousse is sliced.)

Spread a layer of plain mousse in the terrine, filling it by ¼. Smooth out with the back of a soup spoon dipped in cold water. Stir a dollop of mousse into the watercress (about twice the amount of mousse to cress) and spread into terrine, smoothing it also with a wet spoon. Spread on another layer of plain mousse, then remove all but a large dollop of mousse from the processor bowl. Place salmon in processor with the remaining mousse and purée for several seconds until smooth; spread the salmon in the terrine,

A layer of watercress gives its bright-green color to the creamy layers of fish.

and top with a final layer of plain mousse, filling the terrine to the top. Cover with wax paper, buttered side down, then foil—paper and foil should not come too far down sides of mold, or water from baking pan may seep into mousse.

🕐 Assembled terrine should be baked promptly, since raw fish deteriorates rapidly even under refrigeration.

Baking
1 ¼ to 1 ½ hours
As soon as possible, set the terrine in the preheated oven in the pan of hot water. When mousse starts to rise above rim of terrine, after an hour or more, it is almost done—and not until then. At that point, also, you will begin to smell the delicious aromas of cooking fish. It is done at an interior temperature reading of 160° F/71° C—top will feel springy, not squashy, and mousse can be gently pulled away from side of terrine.

To serve hot
Leave in pan of water in turned-off oven, door ajar, until serving time. Cut slices directly from the terrine and serve with the sour cream sauce described farther on, or with melted butter, or white butter sauce (page 110).

To serve cold
Remove mousse from oven and let cool. When tepid, drain off accumulated juices—there will be several tablespoons that you may use in your sauce. When cool, cover with plastic wrap and refrigerate.

Serve this beautiful tri-color mousse on top of—not under—its sour cream sauce.

To serve, cut slices directly from terrine, and accompany with the following sauce. (Spoon a dollop of it onto the plate, place the slice over the sauce, and decorate with a sprig of parsley or watercress.)

🕐 Baked terrine will keep for several days under refrigeration.

Sour Cream Sauce for Fish:
When you are serving a sauce with something as delicate as a fish mousse baked in a terrine, you want a sauce that will go nicely with it but not mask any of its subtle flavors. Go easy on the seasoning here, then, hoping to make it just right for that mousse.

For about 2 cups (½ L)

The mousse cooking juices
1 cup (¼ L) sour cream
2 egg yolks (optional, for color)
½ cup (1 dL) heavy cream
1 tsp, more or less, prepared horseradish
½ tsp, more or less, prepared Dijon-type mustard
Drops of lemon juice
Salt and white pepper

If you have more than about 4 tablespoons of cooking juices, boil them down until they have reduced to that amount. Then pour into a mixing bowl, beat in 2 or 3 tablespoons of sour cream, then the egg yolks if you are using them. Stir in the rest of the sour cream and the heavy cream, and season to your taste with the horseradish, mustard, lemon juice, salt, and pepper.

🕐 Store in a covered bowl in the refrigerator; will keep for several days.

Variation—Sour Cream Sauce with Herbs:
In some cases, minced green herbs would go well in the sauce, especially if you are serving it with plain boiled fish. Stir in minced chives, chervil, tarragon, parsley, basil—according to your particular fish and your own desires.

Pâté en Croûte

Spiced and wine-flavored ground meats baked in a pastry crust

For a 4- to 5-pound (1 ¾- to 2 ¼-kg) pâté, serving 10 to 12 people or more

Although you can form the crust on an upside-down bowl, as illustrated farther on, and you can make it of any size or shape you wish—a pâté baked in its own special springform is particularly appealing because it looks as if it came straight out of a French *charcuterie.*

Manufacturing Notes:
Measuring capacity of mold

To determine the capacity of your mold, set it on a large piece of newspaper or plastic wrap on a tray, and measure into it beans or rice by the cupful. The fluted one illustrated here holds 10 cups (2½ L); the oval one, a little bit less.

Dough talk

You need a dough that will stand up to 2 hours of baking, that will be strong enough to hold up after baking, and yet that will be reasonably good to eat—pâté doughs are not epicurean delights anyway, but should be palatable. Be sure you roll it thick enough, or it will crack either during or after baking, and will be very difficult to line with aspic. (Note aspic layer between top of meat and crust in the illustration: aspic is poured in through holes made in top crust, after pâté has baked and cooled.)

Fat content

A meat pâté is just not successful if you cut down on the amount of pork fat needed to make it tender and to give it the quality it should have. A great deal of the fat renders out during cooking, but if you are restricted as to fats, pâtés are not the kind of food you should even consider in your diet. Fat proportions in classic French recipes can be as high as one to one, or at least 1 part fat to 3 parts meat; I am suggesting that ¼ of the total amount be fat, which is as little as I think one can use successfully.

Pig's caul—caul fat

In most recipes, a thin sheet of pork fat lines the inside of the dough, before the meat mixture goes in. This not only bastes the outside of the meat, but reinforces the crust. If your crust is solid enough, you do not need that extra fat, but I have included a pig's caul lining—mostly because I like to use it, and also to show you that it exists. (See Remarks, page 96).

Dough for Pâté:

For an 8- to 10-cup (2- to 2½-L) springform

5 ¼ cups (¾ kg) all-purpose flour, unbleached preferred (measure by dipping dry-measure cups into flour and sweeping off excess)

1 Tb salt

2 sticks (8 ounces or 225 g) chilled unsalted butter

8 Tb (4 ounces or 115 g) chilled lard

1 ½ cups (3 ½ dL) cold liquid: 6 egg yolks plus necessary ice water, plus droplets more water if needed

---

Equipment:

A heavy-duty electric mixer with a flat beater is useful here

---

If you do not have a mixer of the right type, rub flour, salt, and fats together with balls of your fingers, rapidly, without softening fat, until fat is broken into the size of small oatmeal flakes; rapidly blend in the liquids, to make a moderately firm dough. Knead into a rough cake. Wrap in plastic and refrigerate.

If you have a mixer, blend flour, salt, and fats at slow speed until mixture looks like coarse meal; blend in liquid, still at slow speed, until dough masses on blade. Turn out onto work surface, adding droplets more water to any unmassed bits in bottom of mixing bowl. Dough should be moderately firm. Knead into a rough cake. Wrap in plastic and refrigerate.

Dough should be chilled for at least 2 hours, to give flour particles time to absorb the liquid, and to relax the dough after its mixing.

🕐 May be made in advance, but dough containing unbleached flour will turn gray after a day or so under refrigeration—it keeps perfectly in the freezer, however.

Veal and Pork Filling for Pâtés and Terrines:

For about 9 cups (2 ¼ L)

3 cups (1 ½ pounds or 675 g) ground veal

3 cups (1 ½ pounds or 675 g) lean pork ground with 2 cups (1 pound or 450 g) fresh pork fat*

4 "large" eggs

2 ½ to 3 Tb salt

4 large cloves garlic, puréed

1 ½ Tb thyme

½ tsp ground imported bay leaves

1 ½ tsp ground allspice

1 tsp freshly ground pepper

1 ½ cups (3 ½ dL) cooked minced onions (sautéed slowly in butter)

½ cup (1 dL) Cognac or Armagnac

⅓ cup (5 Tb) dry Port wine

Garnish for Interior of Pâté:

1 cup (¼ L) chicken livers sautéed briefly in butter, or diced boiled ham, or strips of ham alternating with strips of veal, and/or truffles, pistachio nuts, etc., etc., etc.

Equipment:

A heavy-duty mixer with flat beater is also useful here for filling (not garnish)

* *Note:* Fresh pork shoulder is ideal because it contains just about the right proportion of lean and fat.

Beat all filling ingredients together until very well mixed. To check seasoning, sauté a spoonful, turning on each side, for several minutes to cook through; taste very carefully —salt and seasonings should seem almost twice as strong as normal, since they become very much milder after the pâté has baked and

cooled. We found the listed proportions right for us, after a too mild pâté or two—but spices vary in their savor; measurements, as always, are only indications and suggestions from one cook to another.

Fitting the Dough into the Spring-form Mold:

The chilled and rested dough

Flour for rolling out, etc.

A little lard, for greasing mold

Equipment:

The spring-form mold; a heavy rolling pin; a cup of water and a pastry brush; an edged baking sheet or jelly-roll pan

Make a paper pattern to guide you in forming dough cover, later; grease inside of mold.

Pâté en croûte —its rich meat stuffing laced with Port and Cognac, spices, and herbs, all encased in a greatcoat of decorated pastry

The dough is to be formed into a pouch that will fit into the mold so there will not be extra folds of dough. Here is a clever system invented by some ancient and nameless *croûtiste:*

Place the chilled dough on a lightly floured work surface and roll rapidly out into a rectangle about 1 inch (2½ cm) thick, and several finger widths larger and longer than the top and side of the mold. (*1*) Paint short sides of dough with a strip of water, and spread a thin layer of flour on bottom half; (*2*) fold the dough in half and press dampened sides together to seal (flour prevents interior flaps of dough from sticking together).

To start forming the pouch, bend the two sides down toward you, as shown, then roll the dough away from you, gradually lengthening it into a pouch shape. Careful here not to thin out the dough too much—combined thickness of the 2 layers should be no less than ¾ inch (2 cm).

Lightly flour the baking sheet, and place the greased mold upon it when you have lengthened the pouch to the right size. (*3*) Lift the dough into the mold, and fit it gently onto the baking sheet and side of mold, being careful not to stretch or thin out the dough—which could cause leakage or cracks during baking.

Fold edges of dough down outside of mold, and trim off with scissors, leaving a 1-inch (2½-cm) overhang. If by any chance you feel dough is too thin in places, patch with strips of raw dough—painting surface lightly with cold water, and pressing new dough in place.

🕐 Mold may be lined an hour or more in advance; cover closely with plastic wrap and refrigerate.

Roll out the leftover dough to a thickness of about 3/16 inch (approximately ¾ cm). Cut 2 pieces the size of the paper pattern (for covers), and whatever decorative cut-outs you have decided to use. Place on a plate, cover with plastic wrap, and chill.

Filling the Dough-lined Mold, and Finishing the Pâté:

A sheet of pig's caul, or strips of fresh pork fat ⅛ inch (½ cm) thick, to line sides and bottom of mold (optional)

About 9 cups (2¼ L) meat filling—veal and pork, or other

A garniture, like sautéed chicken livers, or other (optional)

The dough-lined mold and decorative dough pieces

Egg glaze (1 egg beaten with a pinch of salt and 1 tsp water)

Equipment:

1 or 2 pastry brushes; aluminum foil or pastry-bag tubes (for funnels)

1

2

3

4

4) If you are using caul fat, drape it into the mold; or line bottom and sides with pork fat, if using.

5) Pack half the meat filling into the mold, press the optional garniture over it, and cover with the rest of the filling, reaching to the rim of the mold.

6) Press one of the cover pieces of dough over the filling, and fold the overhanging edges of the dough lining up over it. Paint with water, and press the second dough cover in place.

Paint top with water, and press decorations in place; press designs on top of the larger pieces with the back of a knife.

With a sharp-pointed knife, make 2 steam holes in top of dough cover, going right down into the meat. Wind 2 bits of aluminum foil around a pencil (or use metal tubes) to make funnels; butter them, and insert in the holes. (Needed to prevent crust from cracking as pâté steams and bubbles during baking.)

🕐 Pâté may be formed and decorated in advance, or may even be wrapped and frozen at this stage . . . thaw for a day in the refrigerator before baking.

7) Just before baking, paint with egg glaze, and make light crosshatchings in the glaze, over the dough, with the point of a knife.

Baking

Oven at 425°F/220°C and 350°F/180°C
Set in lower middle level of preheated oven and bake for about 20 minutes, or until pastry has started to brown lightly. Then turn the oven down and continue baking to an internal temperature of 155–160°F/67–71°C—which will usually take about 2 hours and 15 minutes for a 2-quart (2-L) mold of this general shape. Keep checking every 10 minutes after 1¾ hours, and if crust begins to brown too much, cover loosely with aluminum foil. Juices, bubbling up from pâté, should almost entirely lose their rosy color—being a faint pink at most, or a clear yellow. (Several times during baking, remove accumulated fat with a bulb baster or spoon from pan holding pâté mold.)

When done, remove from oven and let cool—2 hours or so are needed for the meat filling to consolidate itself, and for the crust to firm. After that time you may carefully remove the spring-form mold—or you may leave it on until pâté is cold. Then remove it.

Chill the pâté for 6 hours or longer, covered with plastic or foil. When thoroughly cold it is ready for its aspic lining—which fills the space between crust (where meat has shrunk during cooking) and meat.

🕐 A pâté (without aspic) will keep for 10 days under refrigeration. I do not think a cooked pâté freezes well, and do not recommend it—it has a damp quality when defrosted that cannot be disguised. However, I have not yet tried freezing, thawing, and reheating—it might help!

Filling the Spaces with Aspic:

4 cups (1 L) beautifully flavored aspic (see note next page)

The chilled pâté en croûte

Equipment:

A small-ended funnel or the metal tube from a pastry bag; a bulb baster

5

6

7

Note on Aspic: If you have no home-made beautiful clarified beef or brown poultry stock (page 66), use best-quality canned consommé: flavor it with dollops of Port or Madeira and Cognac to taste. Then dissolve 4 packages (4 Tb) plain unflavored gelatin in part of the cold liquid; when soft, heat it with the rest of the liquid, stirring, until gelatin is completely dissolved and there is not a trace of unmelted gelatin to be seen or felt. Very carefully correct seasonings, accentuating their strengths—remembering that flavors die down when foods are served cold. This is a stiff aspic, befitting an outdoor picnic pâté. Chill half of it, over ice, until cold but not set.

Aspic is now to be poured into the pâté, through the funnel holes; make sure they are not clogged, by poking down through them with a skewer to reveal the meat below. Place funnel or metal tube into one of the holes, and drop down through it dribbles of aspic, stopping now and then to tilt pâté in all directions. Continue until you see that aspic has come up to level of both holes. (Sometimes top of dough has not risen from top of meat, and you will not succeed in making the aspic enter—you may be sure crust has separated from meat in some places, however; you can only try your best to make it penetrate. If you do not succeed, pour the aspic into a pan, let it congeal in the refrigerator, then chop it up—crisscrossing with a knife in the pan—scoop the chopped aspic into a bowl, and serve along with the pâté, as a most pleasant accompaniment.)

To serve a pâté en croûte

How to cut up a *pâté en croûte?* You have to be daring when faced with fancy shapes like the fluted ogival—the one pictured. My system is to cut it in half crosswise with a serrated knife, then to cut the half lengthwise, and to cut each half of that into bias slices. Don't expect the slices to be neat and the crust to remain whole, especially with an edible crust such as this one. The crust may break, and the aspic may separate from the top, but you can arrange the slice neatly enough as you put it on the plate.

🕐   A pâté baked in a crust with aspic filling will keep safely under refrigeration only for 3 or 4 days. If you wish to keep it longer, remove crust and aspic, and wrap meat filling securely in foil, where it will keep several days longer, and will always be welcome as a delicious plain ordinary marvelous pâté . . . or fancy French-type meat loaf.

Another Way to Make the Crust— Upside-down Molds:

If you don't have a spring-form hinged pâté mold, or want to make individual pâtés as illustrated here, a fine system is to form your dough on any kind of handy container that you turn upside down. Prick the dough all over, then set it in a preheated 400°F/205°C oven for 15 to 20 minutes to bake until set and barely browned. Unmold the crust, turn it right side up, fill it with pâté mixture, top it with a raw dough cover and decorations, and bake it as usual. Illustrated here are small pâtés that were baked about 45 minutes. The bottom crust is formed on an upside-down ovenproof jar. When filled, baked, and chilled, you may wish to pour in cold aspic, to fill empty spaces between meat and crust. Make pâtés this way in any shape and size you wish.

Single-serving pâtés

Plantation Spice Cookies

Sugar and molasses spice-ball cookies rolled in chopped peanuts

Variation on an old theme, this type of cookie is sometimes called a spice ball because it starts out round—though it ends up flat. They come in all sizes, but not many have these particular flavors. Easy to make and to bake, they are perfect for picnics or to serve with afternoon tea to sylphlike friends.

For 24 cookies 3 ½ inches (9 cm) in diameter

1 cup (4 ounces or 115 g) unsalted peanuts

1 ¼ cups (8½ ounces or 240 g) sugar

1 ½ sticks (6 ounces or 180 g) unsalted butter

1 "large" egg

⅓ cup (5 Tb) dark unsulphured molasses

2 cups (10 ounces or 285 g) all-purpose flour (measure by dipping dry-measure cup into flour container and sweeping off excess)

2 tsp baking soda

1 tsp powdered cinnamon

¾ tsp powdered cloves

½ tsp each powdered ginger and powdered nutmeg

¼ tsp salt

Equipment:

A nut chopper or grater (blenders and food processors do not work with peanuts); an electric mixer is useful; a flour sifter or a sieve; 2 or 3 large baking sheets, buttered

Grinding the nuts

Because of the peanut's shape and smoothness, it does not chop up evenly in a blender or food processor—you could chop the peanuts first in a bowl and finish in a processor, but that seems like double work. Buy them already chopped, or chop with one of the patent gadgets, or in an old-fashioned wooden bowl with a curve-bladed chopper. They should be in pieces of about 1/16 inch (¼ cm). Reserve half in a bowl with ¼ cup (50 g) of the sugar, for later.

Mixing the cookie dough

Place second half of peanuts in the mixer bowl with the rest of the sugar and the butter cut into pieces; cream together until light and fluffy. Beat in the egg, then the molasses.

Plantation spice cookies crusted with chopped peanuts and sugar

Put flour, soda, spices, and salt into sifter or sieve, and stir to blend; sift, then beat or stir into the cookie dough.

Forming the cookies
Oven preheated to 350°F/180°C
(The cookies are formed by rolling the dough into balls, rolling the balls in sugar and ground peanuts, then placing on baking sheets. If dough is too soft to form easily, chill for 20 minutes or until it has firmed up.)

Spread the reserved ground peanuts and sugar on a sheet of wax paper. With a tablespoon, take up a lump of dough and roll it into a Ping-Pong-sized ball. Roll ball in the sugar and chopped nuts, and place on a buttered baking sheet. (A 12-by-15-inch or 30-by-38-cm sheet will take 9 cookies—they spread as they bake.)

Baking
When one sheet is filled, place in middle (or lower or upper middle) level of preheated oven, fill the next sheet, and place in the oven, then the third. Cookies this large take about 15 minutes, and are done when set around the edges but still soft in the center—they swell as they bake, and the tops will crack. Take the cookies from the oven as done, and in 2 to 3 minutes they will crisp enough to be removed to a cake rack. Let cool.

● To store the cookies, place in a cookie tin or airtight plastic bag, where they will keep nicely for several days. Or, for longer storage, freeze them.

Spice cookies flatten as they bake.

● Timing

There are no last-minute or even last-hour jobs on this picnic, except to pack it, and that's easy if you have enough ice, or an insulated chest.

Your last job, which can be done 6 hours in advance, is to assemble the gazpacho salad. Allow at least half an hour for the trimmed vegetables to drain and to release some of their moisture. As you trim them, you can also trim and refrigerate the crudités.

The *pâté en croûte* can be baked as much as 3 days beforehand; the terrine, too. The cookies can be baked even a day or 2 earlier than that—or bake way ahead and freeze them.

The dough for the pâté crust can be mixed at any time, and so can the breads, if you are making them yourself. Both freeze well.

Menu Variations

Instead of having *gazpacho* in salad form, take gazpacho soup; among other good cold soups are cucumber, beet (page 81), mushroom, asparagus, pea pod, spinach, green herb, celery, zucchini, turnip, tomato, watercress, and vichyssoise. If you're omitting the fish terrine, try cold scallop soup; cold white bean soup is delicious, too. Or, to return to salads, consider skewered vegetable salad, potato salad, or cold braised topinambours, or cold artichoke hearts filled with shellfish or a vegetable mixture, or cold eggplant cases stuffed with mushrooms, or a cold ratatouille.

You can vary the fish terrine by coating it with aspic and serving it unmolded—though perhaps not on a very hot day! You can stuff it into edible sausage casings and serve "fish dogs." You can take along a whole poached fish, like salmon or striped bass, or poached fish steaks, or lobsters. Or, if it's a boat picnic, take hook, line, and sinker, and good luck to you.

Pâté en croûte can be infinitely varied, or served crustless, as a terrine; most books, including my own, are full of recipes. And of course you can stuff a boned bird with a pâté mixture (such as the Chicken Melon on page 22 of *Julia's Breakfasts, Lunches, and Suppers*). You can bake it with or without a crust, and/or coat it with aspic. The crust can be varied too, as in *Mastering II*, which has a pâté baked in brioche dough in a round pan (you cut it like a pie). Going a little further afield, you could serve a quiche, or a noble puff pastry Pithiviers stuffed with ham, or Cornish pasties, *chaussons*, and other meat turnovers.

As for the *cookies,* I do think it's nice to finish off with a crunch! *Mastering I* and *II* both have *sablé,* or sugar, cookies (not sand cookies, as I've heard them called in English; they're named for Madame de Sablé, who invented them in the seventeenth century). *Mastering II* has cat's tongues, almond *tuiles* (fragile again), and two delightful puff pastry cookies; *J. C.'s Kitchen* has *tuiles* made with walnuts, cat's tongues, gingerbread, and two kinds of madeleines (really little sponge cakes—these would be delicious, though not crunchy).

Leftovers

The *gazpacho salad* will keep 3 to 4 days, but does lose a little of its charm. I think it might be nicer served as a soup, either hot or cold, with tomato juice added plus any other flavorful juices you saved when draining the trimmed vegetables.

The *fish terrine* keeps for several days; let's say 3 to play safe. If you have quite a bit, you might unmold it and serve it coated with aspic, as a beautiful first course for a fancy dinner, or turn the remains into a fish soup.

Once aspic'd, the *pâté en croûte* will not keep longer than a few days (see recipe).

On keeping *cheeses:* they vary, but remember to wrap them separately and they'll last much longer in the refrigerator. Cheese molds seem to turn each other on.

The *cookies* will keep for several days in a closed tin, or can be frozen.

Postscript: Picnic packing

Everybody has his own bag of tricks for this cheerful job; here are a few hints.

In case of damp or hard ground to sit on, take a rainproof poncho and a blanket. Our own green treasured blanket has accompanied us on picnics the world over, and is almost a talisman. Take extra water for drinking and hand washing, especially if the dog's coming along, and don't forget his favorite nibbles. We pack a roll of paper towels, extra—and extra-large—paper napkins, and we use insulated chests. If you like wicker hampers, line them with ant foilers (plastic dry-cleaner bags), so that, if the basket is set on the ground, ants can't wriggle in through the crevices. I know families with children who pack light, compact amusements with every picnic, usually in a special box for just that purpose: a bat and ball, a kite, a Frisbee, horseshoes to pitch, cards, and a few books. Tied to one family's playbox, there is a whistle, for calling the children in. And speaking of tying, we've attached a bottle opener and a corkscrew permanently to our insulated chest, on long strings so they need never be detached—and lost. We always take rope or strong string when we plan to feast near an icy stream, so bottles can be suspended in the water—just as they can be lowered over the stern on a boat picnic.

Good gadgets to know about: one is a liquid, sold in metal containers; put them in the freezer, and they get ultracold and stay that way for an amazingly long time. We put a frozen one in the ice-cube chest, to delay melting. On chilling generally: since cold air moves downward, have flat-topped containers on which you can heap ice cubes.

Finally, as always: don't forget the salt!

Appendix

Butter

Butter substitutes

There is no substitute for the taste of good butter in cookery. However, if you are using other spreads, they usually react in the same manner as butter, and you can use them interchangeably.

Clarified Butter:

Since butter is made from cream, a certain residue of milk particles remains in it after churning — more or less, depending on the quality of the butter. It is this milky residue that blackens when the butter is overheated, giving the butter itself and anything that cooks with it a speckled look and a burned taste. Therefore, if you are to brown anything in butter alone, you must clarify it, meaning that you rid the butter of its milky residue. Although you can clarify it by letting it melt and spooning the clear yellow liquid off the residue, which sinks to the bottom of the pan, you are getting only a partial clarification because much of the yellow liquid remains suspended in the residue. You are far better off actually cooking the butter, which coagulates the milk solids and evaporates the water content. Here is how to go about it.

To clarify butter
For about 1½ cups (3½ dL)

1 pound (450 g) butter
Equipment:
A 2-quart (2-L) saucepan; a small sieve lined with 3 thicknesses of washed cheesecloth; a screw-topped storage jar

For even melting, cut the butter into smallish pieces and place in the saucepan over moderate heat. When butter has melted, let it boil slowly, watching that it does not foam up over rim of pan. Listen to it crackle and bubble, and in a few minutes the crackling will almost cease — at this point, too, the butter may rise up in a foam of little bubbles. The clarification has been accomplished: the water content of the milky residue has evaporated, and if you continue to boil it, the butter will start to brown. Remove from heat at once and let cool a few minutes. Then strain through lined sieve into jar. You should have a beautifully clear deep yellow liquid, which will congeal and whiten slightly as it cools.

Clarified butter will keep for months in the refrigerator in a closed container. Scoop out what you want to use, and you may want to heat and liquefy it before using. (This clarified butter is the same as the *ghee* used in Indian cookery.)

White Butter Sauce — Beurre Blanc:
For 1½ to 1¾ cups (3½ to 4 dL)

4 Tb wine vinegar, preferably white
2 Tb lemon juice
4 Tb dry white French vermouth
2 Tb very finely minced shallots or scallions
Salt and white pepper
2½ sticks (10 ounces or 285 g) chilled butter, cut into pieces
Optional additions: 4 to 8 Tb heavy cream, minced parsley and/or dill

Simmer the vinegar, lemon juice, vermouth, shallots or scallions, ½ teaspoon salt, and a big pinch of pepper in a smallish enameled or stainless-steel saucepan until reduced to about 1½ tablespoons. Then start beating in the butter and continue as directed in the preceding recipe, to make a thick ivory-colored sauce. Remove from heat; beat in optional cream by spoonfuls, then the herbs.

You can make the sauce somewhat ahead: omit the cream, and keep sauce barely warm near a gas pilot light or warm burner, just to keep it from congealing. Heat the cream shortly before serving and beat by driblets into the butter sauce to warm it.

Dough

Dough for Pies, Quiches, Tarts, Tartlets, and Flans:
For an 8-inch (20-cm) shell

1¾ cups (8 ounces or 225 g) all-purpose flour, preferably unbleached (measure by scooping dry-measure cups into flour and sweeping off excess)
1 tsp salt
1¼ sticks (5 ounces or 140 g) chilled unsalted butter
2 Tb (1 ounce or 30 g) chilled lard or shortening
5 to 8 Tb iced water
Equipment:
A mixing bowl and rubber spatula; or bowl and pastry blender or 2 knives and spatula; or food processor with steel blade

Measure the flour and salt into the mixing bowl or bowl of processor. Quarter the chilled butter lengthwise, cut crosswise into ⅜-inch (1-cm) pieces, and add to the bowl or container along with the chilled lard or shortening, cut into small pieces.

Dough by hand

Rapidly, so fat will not soften, either rub it with the flour between the balls of your fingers until the fat is broken into pieces the size of small oatmeal flakes, or cut with pastry blender or knives until fat is the size of very coarse meal. (If fat softens during this process, refrigerate bowl or container for 20 minutes, then continue.) Then, with a rubber spatula, blend in 5 tablespoons iced water, pressing mixture against side of bowl to make a mass. Lift out massed pieces of dough onto your work surface, sprinkle droplets of water on the unmassed bits, press together, and add to rest of dough. Finish as in the final paragraph.

Dough in a food processor

The preceding proportions are right for machines with a 2-quart or 2-liter container; a large container will take double the amount. Turn machine on and off 4 or 5 times to break up the fat. Measure out 5 tablespoons iced water, turn the machine on, and pour it in. Turn machine on and off 5 or 6 times, and dough should begin to mass on blade; if not, dribble in another tablespoon water and repeat. Repeat again if necessary. Dough is done when it has begun to mass; it should not be overmixed. Remove dough to your work surface.

Finishing the dough

With the heel, not the warm palm, of your hand rapidly and roughly smear dough out 6 to 8 inches (15 to 20 cm) on your work surface by 3-spoonful bits, to make a final blending of fat and flour. If pastry seems stiff, you can at this time sprinkle on droplets more water as you smear. It should be pliable, but not damp and sticky. Knead and press it rapidly into a rough cake, flour lightly, and wrap in a sheet of plastic and a plastic bag. Chill for 1 hour — preferably 2 hours — before using, which will allow dough to relax while the flour particles absorb the liquid.

Will keep under refrigeration for a day or 2, but if you have used unbleached flour it will gradually turn gray; it is best to store it in the freezer, where it will keep perfectly for several months. Let thaw overnight in the refrigerator, or at room temperature and then rechill.

Dough for Pâtés and Meat Pies:

The following proportions are for ½ pound (225 g) flour, to keep them in line with the previous doughs, but you will undoubtedly want more if you are making a *pâté en croûte* — like the fine pâté baked in a pastry crust in "Picnic." There the amount is tripled, and the dough is made in a heavy-duty machine, which is useful indeed for large amounts. The proportions and recipe are on page 102, but here is the smaller amount suitable for making it as in the preceding directions.

1 ¾ cups (8 ounces or 225 g) all-purpose flour
1 ¼ tsp salt
½ stick (2 ounces or 60 g) chilled unsalted butter
3 Tb (1 ½ ounces or 45 g) chilled lard
2 egg yolks plus enough iced water to make 6 to 8 Tb liquid

Fast French Puff Pastry

Pâté Feuilletée Exprès:
For one 9-inch Pithiviers and 36 or more cheese appetizers; or for a rectangle of dough some 36 by 12 by ¼ inches (90 x 30 x ¾ cm)

Note: Measure flour by dipping dry-measure cups into container, then sweeping off excess even with lip of cup; no sifting necessary.
3 cups (420 g) unbleached all-purpose flour
1 cup (140 g) plain bleached cake flour
6 ½ sticks (26 ounces or 735 g) chilled unsalted butter
1 ½ tsp salt
1 cup (¼ L) iced water
Equipment:
A heavy-duty electric mixer with flat beater (useful); a 1 ½-by-2-foot (45-x-60-cm) work surface, preferably of marble; a rolling pin at least 16 inches (40 cm) long; a pastry sheet (for lifting and turning dough) about 10 inches (25 cm) wide; a pastry scraper or wide spatula; plastic wrap

Mixing the dough
Place the flour in your mixing bowl. Rapidly cut the sticks of chilled butter into lengthwise quarters, then into ½-inch (1½-cm) dice;* add to the flour — if you have taken too long to cut the butter and if it has softened, refrigerate bowl to chill butter before proceeding. Add the salt. Blend flour and butter together rapidly, if by hand, to make large flakes about an inch in size. By machine the butter should be roughly broken up but stay in lumps the size of large lima beans. Blend in the water, mixing just enough so that dough masses roughly together but butter pieces remain about the same size.

The first 4 turns
Turn dough out onto a lightly floured work surface. Rapidly push and pat and roll it out into a rectangle in front of you — 12 to 14 inches for 2 cups of flour, about 18 for 4 cups (30 to 35 cm and 40 to 45 cm). It will look an awful mess! Lightly flour top of dough and, with pastry sheet to help you, flip bottom of rectangle up over the middle, and then flip the top down to cover it, as though folding a business letter. Lift dough off work surface with pastry sheet; scrape work surface clean, flour the surface lightly, and return dough to it, settling it down in front of you so that the top flap is at your right. Lightly flour top of dough, and pat, push, and roll it out again into a rectangle; it will look a little less messy. Fold again into three as before — each of these roll-and-fold operations is called a "turn." Roll out and fold 2 more times, making 4 turns in all, and by the last one the pastry should actually look like dough. You should see large flakes of butter scattered under the surface of the dough, which is just as it should be. With the balls of your fingers (not your fingernails) make 4 depressions in the dough to indicate the 4 turns — just in case you go off and forget what you've done.

Finishing the dough — the 2 final turns
Wrap the dough in plastic, place in a plastic bag, and refrigerate for 40 minutes (or longer) to firm the butter and relax the gluten in the dough. Give the dough 2 more turns, beating it back and forth and up and down first if chilled and hard. Let dough rest another 30 minutes if it seems rubbery and hard to roll; then it is ready for forming and baking.

Dough may be frozen after the first 4 turns, although it is easier to complete the 6 of them before freezing. It will keep, wrapped airtight, for months. Defrost overnight in the refrigerator, or at room temperature.

*If you have bought the kind of butter that seems soft and sweats water when you cut it, that means it is inferior quality and will not make this puff pastry rise as it should. In this case you eliminate the extra moisture by first kneading it in ice water and then squeezing in a damp towel to remove excess water. Then chill.

Mayonnaise

Mayonnaise:
For a little more than 2 cups (½ L)

Mayonnaise couldn't be easier to make if you just remember these points: beat up the yolks well before you begin, add the oil by droplets at first until the sauce begins to thicken; don't exceed the proprotions of 2 cups (½ L) oil to 3 egg yolks; and remember that a turned or thinned-out mayonnaise is very easy to bring back. Here are directions for making mayonnaise by hand, and in a food processor.

3 egg yolks (for a processor, 1 egg and 2 yolks)
¼ tsp dry mustard
½ tsp salt
Fresh lemon juice and/or wine vinegar to taste
2 cups (½ L) best-quality olive oil or a combination of olive oil and salad oil
More salt, and white pepper
Equipment:
Either a 2-quart (2-L) mixing bowl with rounded bottom and a large wire whip or hand-held electric mixer, or a food processor with steel blade; a rubber spatula

By hand
Set the bowl on a wet potholder to keep it from slipping about. Beat the egg yolks in the bowl for a good 2 minutes, until they turn pale yellow and thicken into a cream. Beat in the mustard and the salt, and 1 teaspoon of lemon juice or vinegar; continue beating a minute longer. Then, by ½-teaspoon driblets, start beating in the oil, making sure it is being constantly absorbed by the egg yolks — stop pouring for a moment every once in a while, and continue beating until about ½ cup (1 dL) oil has gone in and sauce has thickened into a heavy cream. Then add the oil by larger dollops, beating to absorb each addition before adding another. When sauce becomes too thick and heavy, thin out with droplets of lemon juice or vinegar, then continue with as much of the additional oil as you wish. Taste carefully for seasoning, adding more salt, pepper, lemon juice or vinegar.

By food processor
Place the whole egg and 2 yolks in the container and process for 1 minute. Then, with machine running, add the mustard, salt, and 1 teaspoon lemon juice or vinegar. Start adding the oil in a stream of droplets, and continue until you have used half, and sauce is very thick. Thin out with 1 teaspoon of lemon juice or vinegar; continue with the oil. Add seasonings to taste, and if sauce is too thick add more lemon juice or vinegar, or droplets of water.

Storing mayonnaise
Scrape mayonnaise into a screw-topped jar and store in the refrigerator — 7 to 10 days.

Turned or thinned-out mayonnaise
If you have added the oil too quickly and the sauce will not thicken, or if it has been refrigerated for some time and the chilled yolks have released the oil from suspension and the mayonnaise has curdled, the problem is easily remedied. Place 1 tablespoon prepared Dijon-type mustard and a ½ tablespoon of the sauce in a bowl and beat vigorously with a wire whip or hand-held mixer until mustard and sauce have creamed together; then, by droplets, beat in the turned sauce — it is important that you add it very slowly at first for the rethickening to take place.

Garlic Mayonnaise — Aïoli:
For about 2 cups (½ L)
This marvelous sauce goes well with fish soups, boiled fish, fish in cold sauces (like the monkfish *pipérade* on page 82), with boiled chicken, with poached egg dishes, with boiled potatoes — in fact with anything that could use a strong garlic mayonnaise to perk it up. And how do you get all that garlic off your breath? Everybody eats it and no one will notice a thing.

4 to 8 large cloves garlic
½ tsp salt
1 slice homemade-type French or Italian white bread
2 Tb wine vinegar
2 egg yolks
1½ cups (3½ dL) strong olive oil
More salt and vinegar to taste
White pepper and/or drops of hot pepper sauce

Equipment:

A mortar and pestle or heavy bowl and pounding instrument of some sort; a wire whip or hand-held electric mixer

Either purée the garlic into the mortar or bowl with a garlic press, or mince very fine and add to the bowl. Pound to a very fine paste with the salt — a most important step, taking a good minute or more. Cut the crust off the bread, tear bread into pieces and add to the bowl with the vinegar, and pound with the garlic into a paste; then pound in the egg yolks to make a thick sticky mass. By driblets, as though making a mayonnaise, start pounding and stirring in the oil; when thickened, begin adding it a little faster and beat it in with a whip or mixer. Sauce should be thick and heavy. Season to taste with more salt and droplets of vinegar as needed, and pepper and/or hot pepper sauce. Store as described for mayonnaise; if it turns, give it the same treatment.

Tomatoes

Tomato Fondue:
Fresh tomato lightly cooked in butter, herbs, and shallots
For about 1½ cups (3½ dL)

So often one needs a little something to go with a vegetable custard, a soufflé, or a boiled fish — something a little bit tart, something not too insistent in flavor, something with a bright color — this very simple accompaniment often fills just these requirements. (If you're doing the sauce in full tomato season, when they're bursting with flavor, of course you don't need the help of the canned plum tomatoes for extra taste and color, as suggested below.)

2 Tb minced shallots or scallions
2 Tb butter
2½ cups (6 dL), more or less, fresh tomato pulp, chopped
4 Tb or more drained and seeded canned Italian plum tomatoes, if needed
Salt and pepper
Fresh herbs, such as fresh basil and parsley, or tarragon; or dried herbs to taste (tarragon, oregano, thyme)

Cook the minced shallots or scallions in butter, in a small frying pan or saucepan, for a minute or 2 without browning. Then add the tomato and cook over moderately high heat for several minutes until juices have exuded and tomato pulp has thickened enough to hold its shape lightly in a spoon. Season carefully to taste. Just before serving, fold in the herbs.

Index